Casting the Runes

CASTING THE RUNES

The Letters of M. R. James

Edited by

Dr Jane Mainley-Piddock

unbound

First published in 2023

Unbound
Level 1, Devonshire House, One Mayfair Place, London W1J 8AJ
www.unbound.com

Letters © the Estate of M. R. James
Introduction and commentary © Jane Mainley-Piddock, 2023

Text design by Ellipsis, Glasgow

A CIP record for this book is available from the British Library

ISBN 978-1-80018-175-5 (hardback)
ISBN 978-1-80018-176-2 (ebook)

Printed and bound in Great Britain by Clays Ltd, Elcograf S.p.A.

MIX
Paper from
responsible sources
FSC   FSC® C018072
www.fsc.org

1 3 5 7 9 8 6 4 2

I dedicate this book to John Adam William Piddock for having to live with a dead man for the last fifteen years, and perhaps more years to come – who knows?

Contents

Foreword

There's something pleasing about the arrival of the uncollected letters of M. R. James. That one so famous for his cataloguing and his, shall we say, *haunting* of dusty archives should have his own correspondence ignored was a curious omission. But here they are at last, beginning with childhood jottings from home and school which fall into the familiar pattern; the scattergun attention of a young boy, listing his school masters – 'Gaergen who has one arm … (pretty fair), Marshall (don't mind him), Bullock (a pig, wretch)' – and then ending with an abrupt 'I cannot find anything more to say.' But then, as James grows older, we begin to see flashes of his native wit and a sly humour. 'Your affectionate offspring takes up his pluma with the full intention of telling you all he can,' he writes to his parents, detailing life at Eton which includes, startlingly, a request to be vaccinated against an outbreak of smallpox!

There's nothing here to suggest that James would become the master of the English ghost story but there are clues in his everyday life as to the milieu – and crucially the detail – that would go on to inform his legendary stories. Rare manuscripts, bestiaries, sale-room oddities and stained-glass windows figure prominently. 'I am thinking of getting to the BM to look at MS,' he writes, tantalisingly. There are postcards from the foreign trips to Sweden and France which eventually provide the settings for 'Count Magnus' and 'Canon Alberic's Scrapbook'. And there's the first appearance of the 'funny servant', a staple of the stories which I always imagine appeared for comic relief and also to allow James full rein to 'do a voice' as he read out his stories on those famous Christmas Eve gatherings. 'I found (Mrs Smith) standing on my window sill today,' he writes, 'trying to get through my window and she said, "This is a masterpiece, sir. I can't shut it."'

Monty James was, by all accounts, a lovely man and there's charming self-deprecation everywhere in the letters – 'Have returned to King's better and am quite well with the exception of a slight receding of the hair' – but of his inner life there is little trace. It's the world conjured here, though, 'pent mid cloister dim', which was to prove so essential to his writing.

Mark Gatiss
London, May 2022

Introduction

M. R. James is the finest writer of ghost stories that England has ever produced. His collected ghost stories, first published in 1931, has never been out of print, and his stories keep getting re-mediated into radio plays, graphic novels and films that continue to terrify audiences all over the world.

It might have surprised James's contemporaries that we remember him today primarily as a writer of hugely original, terrifying ghost stories, as he was a figure of donnish respectability, Provost both of King's College and Eton, Museum Director and Fellow of King's College; and it is difficult to reconcile this list of professional personae with his alter-ego as the author of such horrors as 'Count Magnus'.

While doing my PhD on M. R. James's ghost stories at Aberystwyth University, I wanted to gain an insight into the man as author. So as well as buying a few books on his stories I searched on a very popular online store for a book of his letters and came up with nothing, apart from a book of his correspondence with the widow of his friend James McBryde (Gwendolen).[1]

This was a start, but as for a bigger selection of his letters, still a blank. Apart from there being a gap in Jamesian study, here was also the proverbial gap in the market, and nature abhors a vacuum. I decided to rectify that, as it seems a definite oversight that (unlike such poets as John Keats and authors such as Oscar Wilde) there is no book of James's letters.

Unless they have the means to travel to the dreamlike setting of the Cambridge University libraries and negotiate a library system which can be rather intimidating (with its hushed interiors and the wearing of white archival gloves), the public can't access James's letters. If anyone is inclined to search the shelves of independent or chain book shops or online book purveyors, they will find that everyone else seems to have had their letters published, but alas not poor old James.

The books extant on James are relatively old: Richard William Pfaff's biography on James was written in 1980, Michael Cox's in 1986, Gurney Lubbock's very small offering in 1939 (two years after James's death) and James's own autobiography, *Eton and King's*, in 1926.

Here was an academic and literary mystery. I started making a few enquiries, as I knew that there *were* letters. Checking the pages of the biographies, their footnotes mentioned quite a few, and on various websites the letters were identified as being in the archives of Cambridge University Library, King's College Cambridge, the Fitzwilliam Museum and Eton College, to name but four places where James's correspondence, whether social, familial, or work related, was deposited.

However, academics and their colleges were famous for just casually archiving work, and not cataloguing it, as James well knew – he had made a very good career out of cataloguing the various archives of Cambridge and Oxford, as well as many other religious and museum archives.

Apart from the various issues of the ghost stories and the books mentioned above, there was very little on James, apart from a book of critical essays published by the ghosts and scholars author Rosemary Pardoe and her website (a virtual treasure trove of Jamesian facts and figures that was very helpful in my first few years on the PhD). It was not until the last few years of writing up my Jamesian research for my PhD thesis that published material would start appearing on James: the first complete book was in 2017, by Patrick Murphy on the medieval angle of James's ghost stories.[2]

In 2019 I became aware of a new way of publishing that might work for my fledgling idea of getting James's letters published. Unbound is a crowdfunding publisher, a new idea based on a very old practice, that of the patron. Patrons helped such luminaries as Keats publish his poems, and artists such as Dante Gabriel Rossetti sell his canvases.

In the case of an author, they would pitch their idea to the publisher, and then get their social media followers to fund the book if they had an interest in reading it. I had over 16,000 followers on Twitter who had been following my PhD journey and who were all very big fans of James and his ghost stories. They also eagerly read my blog on James, where I posted the material that had not made it into my thesis. I had also picked up more followers as I had been the other half of the organisational team behind the two M. R. James conferences that we had held at Leeds Library in 2015 and 2016.

However, 2020 was going to be an exceptional year. The previous Christmas there had been rumours of a new flu-like virus that was killing people. Covid-19 started to make its way around the world, and in March 2020 our government, like many, imposed a lockdown on society to save lives. This meant working online, going out only for exercise (one hour allotted to each citizen per day), and all shops, libraries, workplaces – in fact everything – grinding to a halt.

It was a very, very stressful and strange time, and travelling to Cambridge to research and photograph letters was out of the question. Then at the start of October the government relaxed the rules around the lockdown enough for me to get over to Cambridge, and at the start of that month I found myself on an unnervingly empty train (which kept making noises like the girl antagonist from the Japanese horror flick *The Grudge*), traversing the fens on its way to Cambridge, where I ended up staying in a very empty hotel.

The next morning, after getting my breakfast delivered from McDonald's, I was fortified enough to start my foray into the archives of the Cambridge University Library and soon enough I found myself face to face with the overwhelming picture of an archives room, a polished desk and M. R. James's letters sitting on that desk, regarding me back with an unassuming air.

My imposter syndrome decided to kick in just as I put my trembling hand out to touch the letters in their burgundy folders, tied with very old legal string. Then I also noticed that the rumours about James's handwriting were true – it was bloody awful. Never mind the old jokes about doctors having terrible handwriting; this was beyond the comparisons to epileptic spiders, it was almost indecipherable.

This was the start of many months of making jokes about how hard it was to even decipher what on earth James was driving at in each letter, and to provide context to them so that the person reading the book could understand the historical time and the events surrounding each letter. It often took anything from a day to a week for each of the 101 letters here. I hope that you, gentle reader, enjoy my efforts. But I think that it is best to finish this introduction with James's own words on this subject:

'The public, as Dr Johnson said, are the ultimate judges: if they are pleased, it is well; if not, it is no use to tell them why they ought to have been pleased.'

Notes

1. Gwendolen McBryde, *M. R. James: Letters to a Friend* (London: Edward Arnold, 1956); Richard William Pfaff, *Montague Rhodes James* (London: Scolar Press, 1980); Michael Cox, *M. R. James An Informal Portrait* (New York, NY: Oxford University Press, 1986); S. G. Lubbock, *A Memoir of Montague Rhodes James* (Cambridge: Cambridge University Press, 1939); M. R. James, *Eton and King's* (London: Williams and Norgate, 1926).
2. Patrick J. Murphy, *Medieval Studies and the Ghost Stories of M. R. James* (Pennsylvania: Pennsylvania State University Press, 2017).

1:

Early Beginnings: Life at Home and at Preparatory School

To Sydney James

Livermere
Tuesday, 29 May [year undated]

Sydney,

You're very lovely to me, and I'm very loving to you. Princess snaps I want you to have a piece of my seed cake when you come home.[1]

Jakes is going to sow some mustard seeds in my little box.

I wish you a very happy birthday, and many more of them.

Is it from Montie?

Papa says

Keep this note

Notes

1. This is one of the earliest letters that James wrote, and although the letter is undated, it was written before he was sent away to his preparatory school at 11. Judging by the context of this letter and the reference to 'Princess snaps', he is referring to a family dog or a household servant's dog.

Dear Everybody[1]

Cambridge University Library –
Rare Manuscripts, ADD 7480 D6 1-69,
Letters from M. R. James to parents
from Temple Grove[2]

16 September 1873[3]

Dear Everybody,

I am sorry I cannot answer every one of your letters separately though I thank you for them very much. In answer to your inquiries I am in the [inkblot] upper division of the iv class under Mr Prescott I like Mr Prescott pretty well. This is how he goes "Patteson, compare Magnus" / Patteson Magnus Magnicor" "That's it, quite right". As to what I do, I can't very well tell you. As I myself don't know what I am going to do this afternoon.

Saturday is a half-holiday.

Tell papa I will send him the papers as soon as I get them.

This afternoon the singing master got hold of me try if I could join the choir.

He did not say whether I should not.

I cannot find anything more to say.

Give my love to all at home
M R J

Notes

1. 'Everybody' would have been everybody who may have been living at the family home on the date that this letter was received (Livermere then), as James wrote separately to his brother Sydney at his prep school, Haileybury, and brother Ber at school in Aldeburgh, and again separately to his sister Grace (Gracy) and parents, mother Mary Emily and father Herbert, at the family residence.

2. James was writing home in this letter to his parents, after being dropped off at his new preparatory school (Temple Grove) on a Tuesday in September 1873. This letter therefore was one of the earliest letters he actually wrote home. Temple Grove was then in a Surrey village, now part of Richmond-upon-Thames. It was home to roughly 130 pupils – a large community for a small boy of 11 to become accustomed to.

3. This letter was written on a Tuesday, which demonstrates that James wrote regularly to his family from his school, as it was compulsory for pupils to write home on Sunday nights, in expectation perhaps that some boys might have to be encouraged into the act of penning their activities to their relatives.

Dear Mamma

Cambridge University Library –
Rare Manuscripts, ADD 7480 D6 1-69,
Letters from M. R. James to parents
from Temple Grove

[Late September 1873]¹

Dear Mamma,

Thank you very much for your letter and Papa for his. I forgot to thank Gracy for her photo, which I do now very much. I will also answer Papa's question. On the day after I came, Mr Edgar gave me what he called an examination which chiefly consisted of Two lines of Greek & three of Latin, which I didn't think was much examination. I will now give you a list of The fellows in my division. Knox, Davidson Ma, Praed, Grenville Ma, Mansfield, Crummelon, Pattison Ma, Myself, Rice. The weekly order however is quite different; Then I am next the top. Browning is in the class just above mine, That is to say, the third. We do a great many books here; Greek Delectus Latin Primer, Gr Grammar, Wilkins's Exercises Penroses verse book, McCleans Scriptures History, Children's Garland from the best poets Principles, Text book, Cornwell's Geography, Colliers History Edinburgh High-School, French Grammar: Lettes Conversational grammar. That is all I can remember at present.

In regard to French, we have done it Three times, being Taught by a fat little French man, who gets frightfully angry with the boys: I got up to the top of my class – our scheme of work is this: In the morning from 7.30 am to 8.30, breakfast. (8.45 to 10.45 11.15 to 12.30 12.30 – 1.00 drill no work till 4. 4 to 6pm. Tea 7 to 8. We, That is to say, about half-a-dozen boys besides myself & Browning included, went to Kew gardens last Saturday with one of the Masters. We saw

The Victoria Regia and The great Hope-Pole 159 ft high & 250 years old, brought from Vancouver island. Tell Gracy I wish she would send me some good big hard chestnuts, as hard as she can, for everyone wants chestnuts. They make a hole through Them, put Them on a string with a knot at the end & fight [crossed out word, illegible] with them the object being to knock to pieces each other's Chestnut. So Goodbye.

Believe Me ever your loving

Notes

1. This letter mentions 'the day after I came', which can be traced to the first letter James wrote from Temple Grove ('Dear Everybody') to his parents dated 16 September 1873, therefore this date would have been around late September 1873.

Dear Papa

Cambridge University Library –

Rare Manuscripts, ADD 7480 D6 1-69,

Letters from M. R. James to parents

from Temple Grove

October 1873

Dear Papa,

I have some good news for you. I have had a remove and am on the honours which means that you are allowed to go round the grounds and to spend Sixpence at Richmond every week.

Please tell Linny when you next write to her that I wish I could find time to answer her letter. There are several Jews and Greeks here. One of the Greeks is Vlasto [James includes a sketch here of a small head of a man with long curly hair]. I have made him like an old woman in the portrait. Behrens is a Jew. We had exams this week, on the work for last month and I didn't like it. Booth is a booby. Wilkinson major has a bad eye. But I am forgetting myself. I am in the choir. Our work in this class, under Mr Gaergen[1] is Ovid and Nepos and in Greek, Solon.

Hoping this note will interest you,
I am afraid I must remain ever your very affect Son
Montague R James

Notes

1. James misspells his choirmaster's name as Gaergen: it was in actuality Geoghegan (see the forthcoming biography from Professor Darryl Jones, *M. R. James: A Life* (Oxford University Press).

Dear Mamma

Cambridge University Library –
Rare Manuscripts, ADD 7480 D6 1-69,
Letters from M. R. James to parents
from Temple Grove

[November 1873][1]

Dear Mamma,

I think it is your turn to be written to now.

I wonder whether I shall see Gracy up in London.

Exams are coming on next week I send you the exams of last month in case you would like to see them.[2] It is raining though not at all nothing to be troublesome.

I should very much like a few more nibs, and that little plaid covered note-book of mine (Gracy will know it), which contains most of the precious results of my hagiologic research.[3]

Please to give my respects love and dooty to Mrs Pollard.

Thankyou very much for the Bible Educator which arrived safely.

MRJ
LOVE TO ALL

Notes

1. This letter, although undated, was one pinned by James to 'the exam sheets of last month', dated October 1873, so can be placed safely in November 1873.

2. The subjects on the exam sheets demonstrated the kinds of pedagogical areas covered in Temple Grove's curriculum for its boys, so as well as the Latin mentioned in James's previous letters from his prep school, they were taught History (particularly the Norman Conquest), Geography (heavy on capital cities, and the rivers and ports of major cities of the world) and of course the books of the Bible.

3. The last question on this subject area must have delighted James: 'What does our Church say of the books of the Apocrypha?' Perhaps this question helped to fuel an interest that had already taken seed in James's youthful mind, as indicated by the line mentioning the 'plaid covered note-book' that James asks his mother to send him.

Dear Gracy

Cambridge University Library –
Rare Manuscripts, ADD 7480-E5-1-27,
Letters from M. R. James to Grace Rhodes (sister)

30 January 1874

Dear Gracy,

Thank you very much for your letter. I liked the Kitty story very much.[1] The term is eight weeks to-morrow. Will papa fetch me back this term on the 31st March. I like nothing better than hearing from home. I hope papa will be able to come to see me in the afternoon of the 14th as it is a half-holiday. We are not allowed to play the piano here unless we are on the music list. Believe me having nothing more to say for now your loving brother.

Montague Rhodes James

[Row of drawn hearts]

Give my love to Rd and Judy

And everyone else

Maids

[The rest of the letter contains hieroglyphic letters (some sort of secret message between brother and sister perhaps).]

Notes

1. It is not too much to say that James had a life-long affinity and
   fondness for cats as demonstrated in this early letter between
   brother and sister, and in his biographies where in his later life at
   King's he acquired a ten-week-old tabby kitten that he named
   Miss Dorothea Bridget Antigone Celia Muriel Motts (who went
   missing from his rooms). This comment also brings to mind the
   very important relationship that M. R. James had with his own
   succession of cats, for his home, wherever he made it, was never
   complete without a feline presence. In the letters he exchanged
   with Gwendolen, the widow of his best friend James McBryde,
   and her daughter Jane, James often included an imaginary
   dialogue with his cat (which he always regarded as 'a little old
   person'). See McBryde, *M. R. James: Letters to a Friend.* James's cats
   were made into comedic characters, like the cat who entertained
   his friend Sir Henry Roscoe by hanging off the edge of his chair
   and alternately swinging upon it and catching her tail through
   the bars of the chair. But they were also villains that might have
   found a place in the goriest of his ghost stories. In his letter to
   Gwendolen dated 4 March 1913, he wrote, 'My cat is really very
   unprincipled. Of the last lot of kittens, she smothered three by
   going to sleep on the top of them and subsequently ate the
   remaining one: so I have very little to say to her,' (McBryde,
   p.45). Or there was the time that Gracy brought a big black tom
   into the James household and James wrote that his own cat was
   convinced that as he had not announced his presence to her, and
   that as sprat heads had been seen being taken upstairs on a tray,
   he must be a German spy. As the year in which this was taking
   place was 1914, at the beginning of the Great War, I think that
   his cat could be forgiven for being vigilant. What is evident is that
   James enjoyed the company of cats very much and, like T. S.
   Eliot, found them agreeable muses, even to the point that his

favourite way of sitting was on the edge of a chair in his study with the cat taking up much of the space behind him. His life would not have been complete without a cat.

Dear Gracy

Cambridge University Library –
Rare Manuscripts, ADD 7480-E5-1-27,
Letters from M. R. James to Grace Rhodes (sister)

2 October [1874]

Dear Gracie,[2]

I daresay you were afraid my letter was never coming but it is all the same. I will now tell you all the names of the masters, and what I think of them. Beginning with COW otherwise Mr Waterfield (but when the boys speak of him, they always call him cow).[3] Rawlins (don't know him) Gaergen who has one arm (pretty fair) Marshall/ don't mind him Bullock (a pig, wretch) Luckerman/don't know him well) Davy (nice) Prescott (Pretty good) Prior (the writing master and a pig) Hase (nice) (Boudin) the French Master (fair), and I think that is all.[4] The chief news I have to tell you, is that Mr Waterfield took us, one and two others in his carriage to the Zoological Gardens on Wednesday.

We saw the Chimpanzee; and when we gave it a piece of bun it threw it in Mrs Waterfield's face. We also saw the American Darter which swims about under water for the fish the keeper gives it, and some little tortoises not much bigger than that. [Drawing of Tortoise][5] I will keep the rest for for another letter.

MRJ

Notes

1. Date pencilled in by an unknown hand on the original document in the archives.

2. James had the unusual quirk of using the spellings of Gracy and Gracie at different times on different letters when writing to his sister.

3. Mr Waterfield, the headmaster of Temple Grove, was given the nickname 'The Cow', which was really an anagram of his initials OCW (Ottiwell Charles Waterfield): see the forthcoming biography from Professor Darryl Jones, *M. R. James: A Life*.

4. James has again misspelled the choirmaster's name as Gaergen, as per the earlier letter ('Dear Papa', October 1873).

5. The American darter is a bird, commonly known as the anhinga or snake bird, from the warmer parts of the Americas (Britannica.com – accessed 13 January 2021).

2:
Eton Years

Dear Parents

Cambridge University Library –
Rare Manuscripts, ADD-7480-D6-70-175,
Letters from M. R. James to parents from Eton

26 February 1877

Dear Parents,

Your affectionate offspring takes up his pluma with the full intention of telling you all he can. He is well and takes his drinks regularly. He takes his porter into hall and drinks it at dinner.[1] He thinks that on that point you need not be anxious. He has not given the idea up fairly (as he always remembers) but will do so in a few minutes.

I am getting on all right with work so far, have called out for joyeus and am very serene.

Today it has been howling and windy and raining & it is beastly out of doors.

A fellow in the in the V form, at Cornishes, by name Nugent-Bankes has published a book about Eton everyday life.[2] Rather stupid altogether among others he brings in Godding, myself, & e. Rawsons. Worthers who right (in the preface he says If any are certain he sees himself portrayed in this book … I hope he will not be offended by the <u>unconventional likeness</u>!!!!)

In the book he mentions various tradesmen of Eton Merrick, atkins by name & describes a visit to their shops insulting isn't it?

[Best] Rawlins is a good beak to look up to. I like him. He sets good Sunday R's.

Many thanks for all three of your letters, which I received safely & perused with interest.

I got a letter from Sydney on Saturday. I am glad you saw him.

Godding has just returned from day leave. He has had "a break week, up from the [illegible] and ees feeling much better" for he has been residing in an open carriage for about forty minutes in the sands. It has left him feeling less dreadfulike.

I do not think that that Godding gets on very well. I do not think he is going in for finals.

When he said he was not, everybody came round and knew jayeaux. they were so glad he was not going in for trials. I heard him in an awful din.

(I did not express my joy on that occasion).

He has taken to weeping at the least thing now. I don't think of answers.

I hope [Gracy] Gracey is feeling better. But presumably she hasn't yet been out. I did a beautiful beautiful map last week of north Italy. The only faults were that I made too many lines of latitude. But it was very nice job.

I do not yet know how much I got from the Trials for marks. I am going to drop from this hard work.

French next in school. I am pet of Rather a fat beak who said I was "forte" in French and had I ever habite ai France?

Miscellaneous. one of the Dons went out of Chapel last night with his nose bleeding.

B P Chapman preached in the morning. Rev J J Hornby in the evening. A theme this morning, words consisted of "I will wash etc" very fine. Evening and something else. Services altogether very good.

Thynne has been swiped off his ladder

Poor Thynne.

Ever your affectionate

M R James

Notes

1. It might surprise modern readers that James's mother, Mary Emily, would have been pleased to read that her 15-year-old son was 'taking his drinks' (porter or dark beer) with dinner, regularly. However, then, the act of drinking water would have been unthinkable as well as potentially fatal, as they were living in an era when water was drawn from a system that was not treated. Usually it was taken from local pumps, which would have been sources for cholera, typhoid (the disease that killed Queen Victoria's husband Albert in December 1861) and dysentery, among other strains of bacteria. Porter and other beers therefore were widely drunk by Victorians as a safer choice to accompany their meals.

2. The book that James mentions, by 'Nugent-Bankes', was G. Nugent-Bankes' *A Day of my Life, or Everyday Experiences at Eton* (1877), written while the author (an oppidan or a boy who lived and boarded in the town as opposed to at the school) was still a pupil.

    In the letter James dismisses the book as 'rather stupid altogether' and as 'insulting' to the local shopkeepers whom Bankes profiles. However, age, time and distance seem to have mellowed James's outlook on the tome, as in his own biography *Eton and King's*, the now 62-year-old Don pronounces it as 'most truthful and excellent reading' (Williams and Norgate Ltd, p.77).

Dear Parents

Cambridge University Library –

Rare Manuscripts, ADD-7480-D6-70-175,

Letters from M. R. James to parents from Eton

[March 1877][1]

Dear Parents

Many thanks for your letter & ordering of hamper.[2]

I am at present, and have been for some time, first in schoolwork.

Collections are on next Friday. We have had the mathematical part of them already.

They are a sort of general exam at the start of the half.

Nothing particular depends on them. If you do well in them, you get a book.

Ryle is up for a jdiv: at Emmanuel. So is [illegible]. For the time being I fag for S Spring Rice, draw baths and lunch.

Godding is getting most awfully loathsome.[3] It is quite impossible to protect him. He is given to tears and such and goes about with oppidans ... etc. [hole in letter] – not popular just now. He has taken to not working well.

The school concert is on tonight in hall. Today has been a whole holiday for Cokes's cervau. Saturday is a whole holiday confirmation day.

(i.c. [ink splash] is in early school).

Today (Thursday) I rescue the broken thread of my Epistle.

Many thanks for the hamper, which has arrived today. We have begun it.

This afternoon I walked with Wood to stoke poges. The Grays Elegy place. It is the other side of Slough. Wood was at Parrys at the

G.K. Grammar with WhD Boyle. It is a smaller place than Herschels. He went there.

Parry is old and fat very fat.

I saw the very hideous Grays Monument near the church. It is like a workbox on the top of a footstool.

[Sketch of Grays Monument]

I go nearly every day to the castle, and examine St Georges or the "Albert memorial chapel" or the Round Tower. The views superb.
By the way one can't go down in a top hat[4] will you send my ordinary worn hat or shall I get one here. If you send the latter, it will last me several halves. Please say in your next letter the cricket does not start straight away.

I believe it is generally handled by p.o.o. however, then in good time for that.

> With no more today
> But many thanks for letters
> all warmly received
> and with love to all at L.mere

a Ryle
has just arrived

> I am ever your
> affectionate son
> M R James

Notes

1. This letter was in James's second term at Eton, which was his first complete term due to a food-poisoning incident, mid-autumn 1876, which saw him out of school and recovering at home at Livermere, until his return on 20 February the following half (Eton slang for 'term'). It can therefore be placed roughly in March 1877.

2. Another hamper (after the disastrous hamper of 1876 – that caused the sausage poisoning incident, as Grace called it) had arrived and James continued the tradition of 'messing' with a 'few boys at tea'.

3. James certainly was enjoying his time at Eton in this letter, despite 'Godding' being 'most awfully loathsome'. One expects that he was not one of the boys included in James's mess friends.

4. His excursions into Windsor also called for a sartorial change of head gear (as boys were not allowed to wear uniform top hats when visiting the town). He requested that his parents send over his ordinary hat, or if they had trouble with this request, that he might be allowed to purchase a new one (as money was always very tight in the James household, he notes that this purchase will 'last me several halves').

Dear father, & Mother = Parents both

Cambridge University Library –
Rare Manuscripts, ADD-7480-D6-70-175,
Letters from M. R. James to parents from Eton

(Eton College Crest)

[undated]

Dear father, & Mother = Parents both,

I send this line in addition to the very misc line of this morning to say that; as there are 2 cases of Small-Pox in the school (not in college) v. certain have already been vaccinated, already sure is Ryle, also Harmer etc besides the 2 facts that Ryle advised me to write & that I have not been vaccinated since Have been at School; perhaps you might think it right that I should be vaccinated.[1]

If so, please write
Love to all
Your Very
Affectionate
M.R.J

Notes

1. One can only imagine the furore that would have greeted this
short missive (on the heels of, as James termed it, 'a mis
[cellaneous]' letter that he had sent his parents earlier that day).
As mentioned in the accompanying context to these letters, and
in the words of other James historians (Cox and Pfaff), Mary
Emily, James's mother, was a renowned hypochondriac known
for her worries for her brood of children. This letter must really
have caused both his parents anxiety when it was received.

It was sent at a time when – as the *Maryport Advertiser*, amongst
other papers, reported – 'Attention is drawn by the register
general to the fact that the deaths from Small-Pox in London
were last week more numerous than in any 7 days since the end
of July' (Friday 23 November 1877, *Maryport Advertiser*, British
Newspaper Archive.co.uk accessed 29.12.2020).

This was also set against a large anti-vaccination movement
that had sprung up in the wake of compulsory vaccination
against smallpox, as the *British Medical Journal* commented: 'It has
been constantly asserted, that smallpox has become more
prevalent and fatal since vaccination was made compulsory'
(Smallpox and Vaccination Statistics, *British Medical Journal*,
Saturday May 12th, 1877, from bmj.com/content/1/854/586,
accessed 29 December 2021 13.29).

Members of the anti-vaccination movement were particularly
against being told what to do, and the extraction of biological
material from cows which went into the synthesis of the vaccine
was viewed as 'anti-Christian'.

As I sit typing this during the global Covid-19 pandemic and
the accompanying anti-vaccination movement which worries
about potential fatalities from a vaccine that was rushed out in
response, Mary Emily and James's concerns about smallpox echo
poignantly down the centuries, and hold a particular resonance.

Der Johnson

Eton College
July 1881

Der Johnson

I oap as you are kriteweli am wel.[1] Many thancks fore yewer letter as igotto day. Ow is yureddgettin on from the varseraick as marry you was a kramin it with the larst time as I seen yu – I add 2 cards from you some weks back whitch I did nottarnswear.

What dreadful occurance is Donaldson's death? I am going into palpitations at the thought of it. Who do you think turned up in sixth form passage last Monday old Conny Halston in her skinned rabbit they could only stop a minute or two and they were with old Luxmoore when I saw them, and they send love and regards.

I have just been given a work with Archbishop Juxon's autographs and seals in it.

We have some hopes of seeing Lucy and the Parker's down here Tuesday or Wednesday. They stupidly put off coming on Friday and the consequence is that it has rained ever since.

We had some excellent fun on Sunday just. The corps paraded on College fields and we had a loud band in the room where windows shook out on 4th. A real raucous was created of heavy trumpet and flutes and we waited for the general salute and I beat wild harmony simultaneously with my hand, which was quite drowned. I say "we" but I was not there last Monday, only last Thursday before when a less dramatic demonstration had taken place. Ware was wild with passion and demanded an apology a large party went and expressed some little entreaties and he said let us bury the hatchet. Sydney was also wild with rage as befits one recently created a 2nd lieutenant.

Ware said such a thing could have happened anywhere but in college, "and upon my word" found Sydney in deep disgust. I didn't think it could happen: I don't think the dull Oppidan has sufficient sense of humour to appreciate the joke.

The Winchester salute was another feature of last week, when as upon perhaps as Henley occurs this week, and the Winchester match day. Arthur Ryle came down he was very well dressed in fine clothes in a top hat with a rather vast moustache. He is going down to Southold and Stratford shortly. The Winchester people were as usual told off for their hideous uncouth yelling.

Not much else wrong or odd occurred. I must be off to pray. Again thanks for letters.

Fond farewell.
Yours Always
M. R. James

Notes

1. This letter at first reads as nonsensical, but it is M. R. James and his brother Herbert (Ber) talking to each other in the guise of two tradesmen: M. R. James was a grocer called Barker, and Herbert a butcher called Johnson. They formed this pairing in their childhood at Livermere, their family home, and always maintained this imitation whenever they met.

   Even in the brothers' letters to each other the joke continued, with the characters' intense rivalry becoming the butt of most of their encounters. In his biography on James, *Montague Rhodes James*, Gurney Lubbock summed it up well:

   'A jealous and intense rivalry was understood to exist between these two characters; they crabbed each other and made the darkest insinuations; Barker would suggest to Johnson that he tampered with his weights, to be accused in turn of putting sand in his sugar' (p.28).

   This continued for years and was renewed whenever the two brothers met, even when at one point they had not met for years, with Ber's job in the Royal Air Force seeing him posted around the world. When they met again in Nicosia, Cyprus when James was there for his archaeological dig, they once again greeted each other on the pier as Barker and Johnson.

   The greeting in this letter starts in the phonetically rendered working-class accent that the two brothers assumed the tradesmen might have used, with aitches dropped and words shortened. It is also notable that this way of speaking may not have been the actual vernacular used by the working class, but then the brothers' experience of the class system was limited in Ber's experience to the men he was in charge of, and in his younger brother's to the servants he grew up with. So they may be forgiven for this limited world view, given the time and social situation in which they lived.

3:
King's College Cambridge –
Undergraduate Years

Dear Smith

Livermere

2 May [1882]

Dear Smith,

My congratulations on the Trinity scholarship. I was awfully glad to hear of it, though I knew you would get it. I only came back yesterday from abroad or else I should have written at once.[1] But though I saw it in the paper at least on Tuesday last, I had not time to [~~give appreciation~~] write off then!

We have had a delightful time. We have seen Florence, Bologna, Parma, Milan aboard two days on the barco Maggione and crossed the Simplon in doing which, we had the most exciting adventure with avalanches, one of which came right over us and covered us up – we were very nearly carried over a precipice.[2] If you know the Simplon, it was just in the worst part, between the 5th and 6th precipices and I saw in yesterday's paper that the place is impassable now.

I must not prolong this letter. We shall meet I hope on Friday.

I was glad to see Winthrop's place. I hope he did not expect to do more.

Don't attempt to answer this. But accept my congratulations again and believe me

Yours Ever

Montague Rhodes James

Notes

1. I'm not sure if Richard Pfaff had seen this letter of congratulations that James wrote to his friend Henry Babington Smith as he records the holiday that James had in Italy before venturing into this rather treacherous territory of Switzerland. James was holidaying with his brother Sydney, brothers Stuart and St Clair Donaldson and 'others', whom Pfaff doesn't record in his biography of James (Pfaff, p.47). Although the letter is meant to be one of congratulations, James does display the typical default setting of a young man given to enthusiastic bragging of his excitement over a foreign – and, it must be said, rather dangerous – trip.

2. The pass that James refers to is the Simplon, a high mountain pass connecting Brig in the canton of Valais to Domodossola in Piedmont. The villages on either side of this pass (such as Gondo) are actually in Switzerland, which the party had crossed into from their Italian sojourn. Let us hope that James's mother Mary Emily didn't hear of her two boys coming near to losing their lives in the mountains of Switzerland. As she was a terrible hypochondriac, worrying constantly over 'her chicks' (Cox, p.7), this fact would have not been received well.

Dear Father

Cambridge University Library –
Rare Manuscripts, ADD-7480-D6 176-317,
Letters to parents 1882–1889, King's

King's Coll
Wednesday, 25 October 1882

Dear Father

I am afraid this letter has been begun too late for it to come on Thursday but the date will show you my good intentions: and I have hardly had a chance to write earlier today. However, this will ~~be~~ make no difference to the quality of my birthday wishes which you may be very sure [crossed out – indecipherable] are a good deal better than mere wishes as such. All health to you and happiness next year:-

[Ex rest indecipherable crossed out] this ritual tibi seemed um cor tuum et omnes consilium tuum confirmat seems a good wish & [indecipherable crossed out] accordingly I make a wish for you.

I am not sorry about Prescot – now I come to think of it. I never regarded it as ~~very~~ a-[crossed out] reality and ~~it~~ it is some relief to think that no particular change is impending.[1] I have no doubt you will be justified by consequences in remaining and I am sure Mother must be glad.

Since Thursday my commitments have been erratic including Friday breakfast with little break since Thursday evening by two way default at Barings. Present himself Eust Loder and SFC – the usual rag supper veal and we had great sport altogether. Saturday I can't remember. ~~Book~~ excellent reading and tubbing. <u>Sunday</u> a walk to centre in town and SLC where we inspected Peterhouse Christs Emmanuel & Jesus chapels.

Monday a blank. Mathematics & translating paper. Tuesday lectures, lunch & lectures. Evening – lectures. AB & SLC C Beumont & Thomson. The afternoon saw me in the misc: at Grays with THS the sale was bountiful here obtained some good facts about Titus from the book audits.

Today has seen me doing Mathematics & verses & AB Benson for a walk with Boyle in the afternoon towards Impington where we discovered Elizabeth Woodstock's Monument.

Tomorrow afternoon I go to the Lodge & then? To dine with the VP in the evening. Friday and we all breakfast with T Somerwell Saturday with Flaishook whom we met abroad.

I had a long letter from Broadbent yesterday six sheets and another from M Tutor with letter very nice but rather seems a shade scholarly but looks forward to the holidays.

St Clair I haven't seen today and yesterday only tussled with him. Tomorrow I expect I must see him towards lunch time. The Exams seem to be tomorrow fortnight Its very hard to know exactly what to read whether text or introductions. But never having done Iesous or Romans-antic only I feel rather helpless & you must not expect anything.

I have some verses to do and my W Hart to be writing only Pictan continuous ago. Tonight in Nixon's rooms for an hour after hall and we sang fleurs I reached on to the ledgers than the other day. I dined in Trinity on Sunday night with Percival a confrere from East Sheen.

I remember not what I did on Saturday. In university-matriculated early & breakfasted with JB who had a party of 8 and made me take an end of his table. It is an evil thing.

Love to all

Everyone affected

Montague Rhodes James

Notes

1. The opportunity of moving to Prescot in Lancashire was a recent occurrence in the life of the James family. It would have been a much more lucrative parish for Herbert to minister but it came with the caveat that it entailed a move away to much more northern climes than the family had hitherto been used to. Sydney, the eldest brother, was keen, but it was to be turned down subsequently on the grounds of Grace's health. The house, it turned out, was, in Grace's words, 'squalid, and beastly'. At the time Grace's health was an ongoing concern, and many biographies do not directly explain the symptoms of her illness. However, reading the context we may discern that it was something to do with her anxiety, as Mary Emily, always a worrier over the health of the family, tried to arrange a 'rest cure' on the French Riviera, but they ended up in Torquay (December 1882) (see the forthcoming biography from Professor Darryl Jones, *M. R. James: A Life*).

Dear Father

Cambridge University Library –
Rare Manuscripts, ADD-7480-D6 176-317,
Letters to parents 1882–1889, King's

King's Coll
Sunday, 5 November [18]82

Dear Father

Many thanks indeed for the notes, papers and letter. It is a good thing undoubtedly I think, to have something tangible of that sort to form one's reading on – I keep at it, but the field is a hopelessly wide one, for a person who finds comfort in details.

[crossed out illegible] Gracy sent me a p.card to ask them at the station the other day. I had a lecture on. I have ordered her the book she asked for.

They have elected me to the Pitt a nice Eton Institution I think and a delightful refuge for me and indeed most of the Eton Freshmen but not Smith who prefers the union or Hedges.[1]

I have asked HB and SLC to come down on Sunday some time. What sort of time? Nov 19th or 26th?

On Wednesday & Thursday SKJ was over – I dined with him and a party of Lodens and we had some fun. All transformed afterwards and Cecil Bayley greatly sophisticated quite the boys and lush. Barry and Bainbridge were of the party. SKJ seemed well.

On Thursday I finished with GRM and in the afternoon went down to Till St Clair you know stroked the 3rd Trinity. On the first day they rowed his Hall, and beat them easily. On the 2nd day I saw them beat First Trinity and yesterday I again saw them win the whole thing against Jesus. The whole four was Etonian J-3 freshmen.

Ridley – an old hand – rowed Bow Putnam 2 Churchill St Clair as 2 had stroked. It gave me more genuine pleasure than anything for a very long time to see him que. He lunched here today. Tomorrow I hope to go with him & herody & Lawtrey who are here by the way. On Saturday last Lady Donaldson, Miss D, and Miss Brown, came down and stayed til Wednesday, furnishing St C's rooms. I had the pleasure of looking after them during the afternoons when he was rowing. They presented me with some very choice plates and candlesticks, and came to five o clock tea here. I could not leave them for lunch.

I have been reading in Chapel this week and enjoyed it. Wisdom was the book, but it is extra ordinary how little "nun" there is about it after the O.T. either the translation is Hittite Aetenoir or [Hellenic] Alexandrian Greek is commonplace after Hebrew. But I don't believe as Humphre does, that the man who wrote it knew.

P.S I think that R.V. of Apoc: is as God and Vulgar as anything they have done. I did send to Roadbad & HES please don't delay them.

P.sii (Tuesday). May I runup my debt to you a little more. The Pitt subscription. and many others that I have come round make me ask, so could you send me £5 which will see me til the Newcastle[2] is paid.[3]

MRJ

Notes

1. One of the very first things that James did upon entering King's was to join the Pitt Club, which was a preserve of Old Etonians at the time. James thought that there was a 'rift' at King's between Etonians and non-Etonians and an Etonian clique, with the membership of the Pitt club being a focus for this rift. The Pitt Club is located on Jesus Lane in a fine neoclassical building and he spent much of his time here along with people like St Clair Donaldson; in fact, the greater part of his correspondence in the 1880s was written from the Pitt Club.

2. The Eton scholarship James was awarded upon graduation from the college (Eton's most prestigious prize).

3. James's letters home during his undergraduate years were often begun by requests for money or thanks for money already sent to him; being a student at Cambridge (as today) was never cheap, and costs totalling £250 a year (in the money of that time) were perfectly normal, and not helped by the 'pretty fast company' that James kept (see the forthcoming biography from Professor Darryl Jones, *M. R. James: A Life*).

Dear Mother

Cambridge University Library –
Rare Manuscripts, ADD-7480-D6 176-317,
Letters to parents 1882–1889, King's

Pitt Club Crest (Stamp)

Sunday, 17 June 1883

Dear Mother

Yr letter of this week comes late does it not. But the last was up to time, I am proud to think. There have been various features on. I went to the Amateur Dramatic or A.D.C. on Wednesday & saw among other things Cox and Box! Just identical twins – Box and Cox which was very amusing. As Father will have told you I saw the honorary degrees given at the garden party, also on Wednesday there was a band, and it was filled with hundreds of people. Then on Thursday afternoon was our concert. It was the last played concert of the term we had all sorts of nice old glees and madrigals and a good deal of the Macbeth music.

(I hope to be home on Saturday). Early in the day and stay til after the Sunday week, and then off to Stow and come up to Looe after that, or else come back home for a few days. On Friday I don't think anything happened. By the way, the Boat function was on Thursday but I luckily forgot all about it & didn't go. It is very stupid. On Saturday the classical Tripos came out Tatham & the clever Trinity men were in the 1st division of the ref class (there are no senior classics now) Arthur Benson is in the second division along with ~~seven~~ Five of the other Kings Men. He ought to have been in the first division & it was a disappointment. But I expect he'll put in for the Tripos next year and probably J. The degrees are given on Tuesday and Thursday & Friday night lodge will be empty. Don't you think you could make a Lady to come and award me? Tomorrow Herbert Ryle takes an eleven against the Choir boys & he asked me to play, also our one armed & one eyed Dean Nixon by name.[1] I head off from College at the latest 10am to Brighton then on July for the day.

More investigations in the glass of King's Chapel have led to my discerning a prophet's head tacked on to an angel and a small piece of scroll work.[2] I assure you I shall end by writing a large book about the windows illustrated by chromolithography a nice waste of time it would be to take a week off and write a long and elaborate work. The provost's book was Hailey's Eastern Church – I had it before, but no importe. He came to the concert, a great event.

all my love

Your most affec

MRJ

Notes

1. J. E. Nixon was an Old Etonian and a Don of many eccentricities, and indeed lacked one arm and apocryphally one eye. There had been many differing stories in James's time as to how Nixon had come to lose these parts, and in what circumstances.

2. For a more detailed description of James's work on the King's College windows, see Cox, p.69; *M. R. James: An Informal Portrait* (New York: Oxford University Press, 1986), p.69; the forthcoming biography from Professor Darryl Jones, *M. R. James: A Life*; Pfaff, p.55.

Dear Father

Cambridge University Library –
Rare Manuscripts, ADD-7480-D6 176-317,
Letters to parents 1882–1889, King's

January 1884

Dear Father

Many thanks indeed for your two letters: and very many also for paying Levelts bill. You will have all the fol up paper I completed them yesterday – but was then just fleeing out for a walk I shouldn't write as from what I have finished this I am sorry to write up St Clair also I have not yet seen he has just done either or he has found me out. Last week was not a time for writing letters. I don't think I am in the lead this time, but don't anticipate any improvement on last year far from it.

Walter Durnford has been up. He came to breakfast with me on Monday. Vaughan of Eton came to Luncheon Sunday. I hosted Hedger at tea today. He has some lovely rooms in Pembroke same set of rooms Pitt had when there. Panelled and well furnished with two chairs. Janet a Ransome of Ipswich here today who played the fiddle. He was the nephew of Gross a solicitor in Bury. Perhaps you know more of him: Trinity people are mostly up – came up yesterday.

Janet Rd Peithetairos got their sheets today the Oopoe has been put to enthusiastic use as it lives on as its cowl has furnished his rooms well.' The letter you forwarded me the other day was 2 sheets from Cecil Barry who does not appear to have left behind his Chicken Pox and has arrived for the scholarship. He forgot all about it until the evening before and came down by an away train.

He telegraphed for his tyf then had on a cap and gown and came up to the Senate house thirty minutes late and gave in a Latin essay and an explanatory letter to the examiners on Ovid. It's for an Ovoid which oddly enough I found an entry for it called an ovate in a frequently examined book today. I don't quite know what it should look like but it was miscribed and is perhaps a domed roof: or a clay object. The soft thing was silk stockings left at Hawsted.

With characteristic accuracy – I when in loci letter – as writing, the post will escape my notice –

Writing more

Yr affect MRJ

Notes

1. Every autumn a Greek play was performed at Cambridge and the choice for autumn 1883 was Aristophanes' *The Birds*. James played the longest part, that of Peithetairos. However, not all were pleased by this turn of events: his father Herbert in particular worried that too much immersion in these extra-curricular activities would distract his son from his studies, and looking at this particular letter he seems to have been right. James does seem to be concerned about his translations of his papers, seemingly 'dissatisfied' with his performance at that time. The old costumes for the play seem to have amused him and his friends however, with the Hoopoe's comb gracing his friend's rooms thereafter.

POST OFFICE TELEGRAPHS

Date — 9th February 1884   Charge to pay — 1d

Handed in at the   Received here at

Cambridge Office at — 3pm   3.20pm

From — Mr M R James   To- Rev James, Livermere

Rectory, Suffolk

The weather is fine but showery the chancellors medals
are got by Leath and Adam and the Craven by James[1]

Notes

1. James won the Craven scholarship, which had been founded in
   1649 and was perhaps the most prestigious of Cambridge
   classical scholarships. It paid (at that time) £75 a year for seven
   years, which, as James was always writing to his parents for
   money (see previous letters), must have been a relief as well as a
   prestigious gain. Hence he sent a more expensive   telegraph
   rather than the usual letter.

Dear Father

Cambridge University Library –
Rare Manuscripts, ADD-7480-D6 176-317,
Letters to parents 1882–1889, King's

Pitt Club Crest (Stamp)

12 May 1884

Dear Father

Many thanks for your last. I should like very much to send a
cheque for husts. I wish to do so on the first opportunity. I am very
sorry to hear they are so ill off. I have very little news. I have long
ago finished Linneas which is certainly hard & Critias, and several
other things. I continue to think that Cicero de Finibus is the worst
book. I'm very sorry for the Provost's death though one knew it was
only a matter of time.[1] I very much wish to know who will succeed
him. I should think he had done enough for the place as anyone of
late years.

I hope you will get through your work all right it is rather offensive
in terms of heat right now. I have been doing writing for some days
now, improving it and my grammar. I don't think it is improving
much according to M.Tutor. We had the heads march with
tremendous effect yesterday afternoon. Mrs Hedger has had a quinsy
& has gone down to the seaside to recover her health. Janet had
people up here the other day.

Everyone else is well I think. I have not heard from Sydney lately.

I wish I could find more to tell you Miss Motts is well and is loved
by all Mrs Smith Included.[2] [the whole] The latter's language I shall
explain, I found her standing on my window sill today trying to get

through my window and she said "This is a masterpiece Sir I can't shut it" meaning I suppose that it is too much for her.

With my love
affec
MRJ

Notes

1. Upon the death of the Provost of Eton, Dr Goodford, the question arose as to his successor. This subject was of some interest to James, who wanted the favourite Dr Hornby to succeed Goodford automatically. Although there was some jollity on the part of some of James's friends that a lay man like T. H. Huxley or a man like Oscar Browning should get the position, Hornby was duly awarded the job on 1 July 1884. (Cox, p.74).

2. Miss Motts was a ten-week-old tabby kitten, acquired by James in the spring of 1884. Her full name was Miss Dorothea Bridget Antigone Celia Muriel Motts and she was awarded a sleeping place in his litter bin swaddled in flannel. She often accompanied him around Cambridge perched on top of his hat. However, unfortunately for James, the kitten went missing from his rooms a few weeks after this letter.

Dearest Pa

Cambridge University Library –
Rare Manuscripts, ADD-7480-D6 176-317,
Letters to parents 1882–1889, King's

King's College Crest (Stamp)

15 June 1884

Dearest Pa

Many thanks for your last. It is a Class I & IV II. I think of coming home on Thursday after the degrees. I don't know that Monday would be absolutely the best day for you. Cambridge would be rather crowded in consequence of this Australian Match: and rather a crush & people will be about everywhere. I do not myself contemplate going to the match, ~~but~~ in fact am far from going to. But it will be rather a bad day for the place I should say as being the tail end of the May festivities.

I think I am to start up, check then perambulate their devices on Tuesday.[1] Childers & I should like to start at the end of the week. But it is not certain if we shall be able to get the machine we need before Monday week. ~~However~~ Childers has been decent aiming particularly in London about the adjustment. We shall all have to pay very much for it on entering France I fancy, and what we do will be refunded on our return.[2] I had to borrow funds from Sydney to go away as couldn't get my savings til August.

Love to all
ever yr eff
MRJ

54

Notes

1. Cycling as a mode of transport was always a large feature of James's life from the start of his time at King's as an undergraduate and beyond. We first find him engaging in this activity in his first (Michaelmas) term at King's in 1882, when he had his first lessons on riding a bicycle (a high bicycle or penny-farthing) and he was almost put off continuing to learn this useful way of getting around. As Cox noted, James was rather pessimistic about his chances of continuing to ride a bike: 'The man held me all the time. I am certain I shall never learn it' (Cox, p.54).

2. Holidays in Europe, often by a combination of trains and cycling, meant that James and his friends could see much of the beautiful countryside before the advent of the Great War, and were the principal means by which James engaged in his favourite pursuits of church architecture and sightseeing.

4:
The Young Dr James – Fellowship of King's/Director of the Fitzwilliam Museum/ Dean of King's

Dearest Pa

Cambridge University Library –
Rare Manuscripts, ADD-7480-D6 176-317,
Letters to parents 1882–1889, King's

King's College Crest (Stamp)

[April–May 1889]

Dearest Pa

Many thanks for letter. I do hope that Ma is pretty clear of the influenza and you too if you have had a touch. I am included in that but believe it is a mild form this year. The people who have had it all have not been left like I was with it. The Victoria Plums have just arrived many thanks to Mother! I shall expect a jug of the juice.

The identity of the deceiver who has been conniving in everything but holding no opinions is E. C. Marchant a fellow of Peterhouse you can judge for yourself of his taste!

There is a new Uncle Remus.[1] Haven't yet succeeded in getting a copy. I am thinking of getting up to the B.M. tomorrow to look at a MS. Today has been foul.

My epistle extends no further than this today. Most of which has been an appeal in church.

Ever yr loving
MRJ

Notes

1. *Uncle Remus* is a collection of folktales of African-American origin narrated by a freed American slave (the 'Uncle Remus' of the title). The tales were collected and adapted by Joel Chandler Harris and first published in book form in 1881. The tales were meant to represent the struggle in the southern United States, especially of the freed slaves on the plantations after the American Civil War and their resettlement. James was always a keen lover of the folktale form, and also loved stories from varied authors such as the fairy tales of Hans Christian Andersen and E. T. Kristensen.

Dear Mr Hurley

Cambridge University Library –
Rare Manuscripts, ADD-7480-D6 176-317,
Letters to parents 1882–1889, King's

King's College Crest (Stamp)

22 May 1889

Dear Mr Hurley,

My syndicate has done its best. It is willing to spend £400 but not more than £180-200 on any one lot & I have selected four lots that I can bid for.

The Bestiary (no.12) The Benediction (No.5) the German "Breviary" (No.6) & the genealogie de la Vierge (No.20).

I don't know if we are likely to win anything [for this] or whether it is ridiculous to attempt it. I am quite prepared [now] to return empty handed.

I am coming to the sale myself. But if we only have the advantage of the help you kindly offered it will be extremely acceptable.[1] I have never been to one of these big sales yet, & there may be etiquettes or fashions with which I am not acquainted. [However,] Anyhow I thought I would let you know what kind of bids we were going to make.

Believe Me
Yours Sincerely
Montague Rhodes James

Notes

1. James was always rather frustrated with the budgets at the Fitzwilliam, King's and the University Libraries. He felt that in comparison to the other 'Oxbridge' university, Oxford, the sums spent on acquisitions were pitiful: viz the Bodleian Library at Oxford was graced with a much larger buying power, and he had to bargain with the syndicates of the various libraries and his own museum to be able to acquire even modest items. In fact he considered the budgets 'timid' (Pfaff p.208).

My Dearest Ma

Cambridge University Library –
Rare Manuscripts, ADD-7480-D6 176-317,
Letters to parents 1882–1889, King's

King's College Crest (Stamp)

2 June 1889

My Dearest Ma,

Many thanks for your last letter. You have now some hot weather
& I hope you like it. I have been pretty busy of late. I daresay Gracy
will have sent you my letter with a tract of the Hamilton Mss in it. I
don't know if I will write it all out again anyhow as this is a
particularly hot evening.

Waldstein talks of resigning the Fitzwilliam but this you will have
heard from Father. I expect probable Middleton will stand. I don't
know about the assistant.[1] Last Sunday I was at Elstree and very
charming it was. This time I saw Ted Sanderson a very fine man
in rather great health. It was very interesting to see the machine
in full swing. There are about 140 boys and some 15 masters.

I daresay I told you about the chapel & so on. I have got a place
to put the window in, which I think is likely to come off. I want it to
be the Good Shepherd.

What else have I done? I have had a great many extremely
pleasant evenings. Dined with Walter Durnford, seen Sydney,
lunched with O.B. today who arrived with Ross, & don't feel impelled
to make his acquaintance.[2] Dinner also with Herbert Ryle & met
Ethel & Mabel Walker, I observed that he and Ethel really get on.

The apex of great function is that of term dance. The ladies will
be presented and Mrs Ryle to put them up and Ethel Walker to

accompany them. It will be a good deal of a family affair, Sanderson, Butler, The Walkers, Ford and I suppose more of them. The main function chiefly is Mays, the date is Friday 11th and Mrs R will help them for Wednesday night, if they would do that there need be no difficulty if you don't mind & I believe it will do them good.

I am sorry that this letter is so untidy. Francis has been playing about a good deal with pen and paper, so that explains it.

much love

ever yr affect

MRJ

We will be a good deal disappointed if the young ladies don't come

Notes

1. James's relationship with the Fitzwilliam Museum was to be a long one. Charles (later to be Sir Charles) Waldstein was his teacher for his Tripos exams, in Michaelmas 1884, but James had already been making a study of the Mss catalogues in the Fitzwilliam before this. Waldstein was already director of the Fitzwilliam at the point of this pedagogical exercise, and it is not clear in any of James's biographies which came first: James's study in the manuscript collection at the Fitzwilliam or Waldstein's tutoring. Whichever it may be, James certainly impressed the older man enough that he asked the Fitzwilliam Syndicate to appoint James as (part-time) assistant director (at the young age of 24).

Within two years of James's appointment, Waldstein accepted another position, that of head of the American School at Athens, and resigned his post at the Fitzwilliam (as James writes in this letter). John Henry Middleton was at that time the Slade Professor of Fine Art at Cambridge, and although James enjoyed his colourful company he was more reserved when it came to the man being put in charge of his beloved Fitzwilliam. James therefore took the unusual step of trying to stand for director himself, but Middleton was appointed in the end.

2. According to all of the biographies, the relationship between James and Oscar Browning (O. B.) was always a fraught one. The character introduced here as 'Ross' was Robert Ross, a young Canadian journalist on the Cambridge magazine *The Granta*. Ross had offended many of the Eton clique at King's by writing an article celebrating a faction of anti-Etonians (egged on by Browning, whose time at Eton was not as pleasant as James's). This subsequently earned him a dip in the college fountain by some of James's friends (Ted Sanderson being one of them). Ross was not someone whom James would have had as a member of his friendship group, being an Aesthete (he was later to be in Oscar Wilde's circle) and very much an outsider.

Dearest Sydney

Cambridge University Library –
Rare Manuscripts, ADD 7480-E3-1-7,
Letters to Sydney, King's

Livermere Rectory, Bury St Edmunds
16 August 1889

Dearest Sydney

"ττβλλζρετςεδ"[1]

Gracie has developed a touch of Rheumatic Fever, and will not be able to socialize today.

ιαπβ:χζήεακίαη at present

So I absolve you from all extraneous generalities and am also ve sorry to tell you that Fr has also fallen.

She is better: but will need a deal of healthful confinement.

With love
MRJ

Notes

1. James was often prone to using Greek and Latin script in his letters, which to the casual eye seems very studious and erudite, often also scholarly. But this is also his idea of an in-joke with his father and brothers, as the usage is often a mix of mangled 'pidgin' that doesn't really mean anything. The Grecian script used in this letter to Sydney is, according to my translator, indecipherable, perhaps lost in translation to borrow a more modern pun. Perhaps its use was meant for their eyes only as some form of code, impenetrable to us as being outside their family circle.

My Dearest Gracy

Cambridge University Library –
Rare Manuscripts, ADD 7480-E5-1-27,
Letters from M. R. James to Grace Rhodes (sister)

2 October 1899

My Dearest Gracy

Thanks for the box. It arrived in time for our Sunday tea, an abundance in particular on Sunday. Last week & the week before was one mass of meetings a lot of work for one. Three days while Father was here. Fri, Sat & Sun. I was enraged to miss out. However, I did see a fair amount of him & thought he was enjoying himself. One of the nights I was at a meeting with G. Duckworth who is an envoy & my age at Trinity. He is quite unaffected.

This Sunday Lubbock was up as well as O. Smith and Luxmoore. Hope we will continue this idea of keeping Xmas here. On the Monday we had a meeting from 11 to 2.45 without a break. A deficit of £950 in the kitchen accounts for this term. Nixon full of threatening bluster. We have an idea of keeping Founders Day on the actual date for once. Because of the War.[1] I would really be rather glad. Partly because it seems a trifle inappropriate to be celebrating & partly because I would like a change.

Much love
Affect yours
MRJ

Notes

1. Because of the mediation James had offered to both warring sides during the 'Robert Ross' affair (see letter 'My Dearest Ma', 2 June 1889, King's), he had been elected to a deanship at King's in November 1899. As a junior dean his duties were not administrative but rather disciplinary and pastoral in nature, with particular emphasis on the areas of King's College Chapel, services and its choir. While he liked this side of his duties, he disliked the association of his new office with the May balls, and the disciplinary side which meant that he often had to confine (or gate) undergraduates to college for a specified time for offences they may have committed. Founder's Day was always a particularly tricky time for the Deans, held on 6 December each year to celebrate the feast of St Nicholas, the patron saint of King's College founder Henry VI. It meant that the undergraduates were often noisy until the wee small hours, interrupting the lecturers and other staff (including here one suspects the Deans themselves). James was relieved when the advent of the Second Boer War (1899) meant that they could omit this celebration (for reasons of propriety).

My Dearest Ma

Cambridge University Library –
Rare Manuscripts, ADD 7480-D6-318-416,
Letters from MRJ to his parents, 1890–1899

King's College Crest (Stamp)

3 February 1890

My Dearest Ma,

This is merely a line to serve two purposes. The first is my best love & wishes for your birthday. The second is to thank Gracy very much for the cushion which I sit upon every day.

The third is to say that Father will have told you I have had the Hypothermia & that most other people are getting it shortly.[1] I think however, that with this clear weather it will start to abate.

I really have nothing else to tell you. I am out & about again at last. Getting up early to chapel & all. I have rather few then two weeks more of full work then Cooke is in charge, and I hope to be freer & get a little sensible work done. The rest of Saturday at a college library, then rest of the week in my room.

Very much my love
ever yr affect
MRJ

Notes

1. When it came to James's mother, his letters always mention his health and he takes particular pains to set her mind at rest. In this letter the mention of 'Hypothermia' must have worried her. James's biographers mention that her maternal instincts towards, as Cox terms them, 'her chicks' were strong but that she never smothered her children with these concerns (Cox, p.7).

My Dearest People

Cambridge University Library –
Rare Manuscripts, ADD 7480-D6-318-416,
Letters from MRJ to his parents, 1890–1899

May 1890

My Dearest People,

I am seldom worried, at least not on my own account. Have returned to King's better: and I am quite well with the exception of a slight receding in the hair.[1] We are more than half way through the term, but all the work is the same, Balls etc. Kings is to give a ball, a large ball ... does Gracy think of coming: if so I believe the Ryles could be found to send her off. They said so. If she doesn't come, I should like to know. I suppose there will be 300 people but I don't know. The college will be quite acceptable, I know that. I daresay I shall have some supper but I don't expect any satisfaction from it.

I lunched on Sunday: Williams asked me this morning to finish his Levant paper again. He is addressing some society on Jewish matters. I have had several odd jobs lately, getting a Coptic paper from a British Museum candidate was one. He is a cousin of Walter Crum's and is a good bright prospect. Tripos on Monday week.

I propose to spend Saturday to Monday at Eton with Sydney. I have had my abscess lanced & it doesn't bother me. Babington Smith turned up last Tuesday & Wednesday & spent the nights with me of which I was very glad. He is considering a living (N. Worcestershire) but Fagan's he has no chance.

Next week is moderately full: meetings in the early part of the week are many but next part I shall have done with at least two of my special boards. Last week I carried a proposal through the council to have all the kings windows photographed.[1] The thing will be difficult but well worth doing. We shall have to have a scaffold (with which The Fitzwilliam will supply us I think) & photograph the windows of each bay on either side from it. Then I suppose J. W. Clark & Middleton & Self will write the text between us.

I was dining in Pembroke the other night & met a wise man called Lord Hatherton. He has a good Bell House in Staffordshire, which he asked me to come and see. Two generations ago they found £15,000 bricked up in the wall supposed to be of Tu Wang of the rarer period.

The clerical Tripos has begun. We shall have hardly any red claret in Hall I. But I hope some will remain for Hall II.

Ever yr loving

MRJ

Notes

1. Poor James always suffered with his teeth, 'from his earliest
   years', and this abscess he had to have lanced is (according to a
   cursory search on the internet's medical pages) due to inadequate
   maintenance of one's teeth (see Pfaff, p.404). In his later years,
   advances in dentistry meant the final extraction of his teeth and
   a set of dentures fixed, which he kept often at the side of him on
   his table with 'a handkerchief' covering them (p.405).

2. The glass in the windows of King's College Chapel had been a
   source of fascination for James as far back as his undergraduate
   years. At that time there was no actual text or complete
   information on their provenance or history, and he started a
   notebook to record his thoughts, with a view even then of
   publication (see Pfaff, pp.55, 96–7, for a full history of James's
   involvement with the glass of King's College Chapel).

My Dearest People

Cambridge University Library –
Rare Manuscripts, ADD 7480-D6-318-416,
Letters from MRJ to his parents, 1890–1899

Pitt Club Crest (Stamp)

2 July 1890

My Dearest People,

Pray silence. Where shall I begin? The term has been altogether
uneventful. The worst diverting thing naturally has been the death
of Miss Buern, for which we are and must be very, very sorry. I am
sure she would have made an appreciable mark on the world had she
lived. Quite recently she had written a very good article – unmatched
in the 19th century on Domestic Servants. Her efforts have impressed
some here.

I have many things to thank you for, addresses, Blackberry Jam for
tea time, and never wrote a birthday letter to my dear Father: which
are calamities aplentiful. I have been busy enough that I work and
keep a somewhat late hour & I hope next term will be quiet.

I am now in charge of the choir quarterly vaudeville to which I
have had the hall where Mrs Bruce denied her tenant rights.[1] It's a
pity as it was an ideal hall for a short performance & It would have
made an excellent music room.

I should think about the Greek play: I have got some tickets for
Saturday – or rather applied for them. Hogarth is coming up that
day & I should remember to thank him & other people for efforts.
For no one helped more than him for only one performance.

The acting speeches are in Hebrew & will be ready soon. I hear that the music is good. It has been a very rough day & I can't write more, & I must go now to chapel.

Ever so sorry

MRJ

Notes

1. James's duties as junior Dean brought him into contact with the choir school, and into the planning of its entertainment and plays. These plays were often written by James himself and performed at various halls (when one could be found), often on the Amateur Dramatic Club (ADC) stage or elsewhere, which would explain the tussle with the hall's administrator here. Two plays written in the 1890s were *The Dismal Tragedy of Henry Blew Beard, Esq.* (with James in the title role) and *Historia de Alexandro Barberio et XL Latronibus.* The action of both plays was Grand Guignol in style with the climax of Alexandro Barberio involving the slaughter of Cassim (off-stage) and his remains packed into a suitcase, the opening of which at the encore gave James a particular delight: 'The opening of this suitcase … I take to have been another of the memorable moments of the play' (Cox, p.95).

My Dearest Parents

Cambridge University Library –
Rare Manuscripts, ADD 7480-D6-318-416,
Letters from MRJ to his parents, 1890–1899

Pitt Club Crest (Stamp)

2 August 1890

My Dearest Parents,

Many thanks and much love to you both, to the one for the cushion the other for the Bible and both for wishes.[1]

I spent Monday to Friday at Chawton house Alton Hampshire, the abode of Cholmeley Austen Leigh where Sydney was billeted, a charming Elizabethan & panelled house & a garden like the back kitchen garden. In the village is Jane Austen's Cottage where she wrote Mansfield Park.

I went to White's Bell house & found it a very good place. It is a fine village flanked by a hanging beech wood on a chalk hill, handy. By the way I spent a kings shilling with Yorke, Benson & Barker going there on Saturday.

It is very well worth seeing certainly the fern house is excellent. On the Sunday we attended a tea for Margaret D of Lincoln Churches & in the afternoon walked over to the castle a couple of miles off. The castle and church are both very good Norman buildings. The white of White's house was so faded that one saw nothing of it.

I hope to join you in town on Tuesday, I hope that it will be fine – I am glad to hear that R C Bosanquet is coming.

This morning I was down to breakfast with R [indecipherable] of Christs, D & G Davies and Rendel Harris, The Wallis Hanmer party

& altogether we are to erect a plan of a series of biblical and patristic studies, a sort of oeuvre that would appear at regular intervals & contain texts, articles and lithographs. Too short for a book & too long for a paper. I hope it will do to give laymen the testament of Abraham – just.

There are few people here, Benson went today.

ever yr loving

MRJ

p.s. The cushion of a splendid set will I hope help me to cover the chairs

Notes

1. As James's birthday is 1 August, this letter is a thank-you to his parents for their gifts, and to update them on his activities and plans for the immediate future. The family seem to be in the habit of gifting their son and brother cushions, as Grace had given him a cushion in the February preceding this letter (see letter 'My Dearest Ma', 3 February 1890, King's). The cushions, it seems, were to be a set to cover his chairs with.

Dearest People

Cambridge University Library –
Rare Manuscripts, ADD 7480-D6-318-416,
Letters from MRJ to his parents, 1890–1899

Pitt Club Crest (Stamp)

[March 1891]

Dearest People,

A busy week. On Tuesday we elected Loring a fellow. I am sorry for Lionel, but luckless artifice demanded this. On Wednesday we examined selected choral scholars. On Thursday choristers, on Friday we looked over chapel. On Saturday we had last council for the term.

Next week as far as I can make out will be chiefly spent in chapel. I thinks of leaving then on Wednesday but my plans have changed. I can't spend the time in the necessary company to go as far as the South West of France, so I have turned my attention in other directions, and my present idea is to go where I can think – altogether in order to get any right paper done & have some right change of scene & therefore go to Antwerp etc, journey the Meuse, & aim for about a fortnight.

My company if it is decided will consist of Benson (perhaps 2), L J Crum and Yorke. How many of them will leave Aldeburgh is uncertain, but I think Benson, me and 2 others. If nobody will, I shall go. I mean to stay at The White Lion.[1] I don't expect I am about before the 4th of April. I may probably look in on you first but that depends upon my paper.

Ever yr loving
MRJ

Notes

1. Aldeburgh and The White Lion were among James's (to forgive a pun) regular haunts. He knew the town from early childhood as he had a family connection with the location, his paternal grandfather having given it a cast iron pump that stands to this day beside the town steps (Joshi and Pardoe, p.41). James spent a week or two at the town's public house and hotel, the White Lion, in April or May nearly every year from 1921 until 1935, the year before his death. Indeed, his story 'A Warning to the Curious' is set in the fictitious town of Seaburgh, a thinly disguised version of Aldeburgh, where his unnamed narrator and the story's other protagonists – Henry Long, the unfortunate Paxton, and the guardian of the Saxon Crown the villainous William Ager – play their respective parts. The White Lion was renamed the Bear for this purpose.

My Dearest People

Cambridge University Library –

Rare Manuscripts, ADD 7480-D6-318-416,

Letters from MRJ to his parents, 1890–1899

Pitt Club Crest (Stamp)

8 March 1891

My Dearest People,

I am glad to hear fair accounts of you. But I have not much time to answer them in. I have a busy week of setting papers before me & Rawlins dimitte employments. I am much interested in the Honnington Wood story.[1] These things always have a small grain of truth. I should be very unwise to believe it unequivocally, that and I frequently have to walk that way at six o' clock in November.

The Brent Eleigh Mss are the latest set of Mss finally decided upon.[2] I have made an offer; I am waiting for acceptance or rejection. I cannot stop the midst of a feueral fuss of beurocrats, but I know there was something I was to say etc, I plan a break to go to W.France Auch & Comminges if I can & come back by Bordeaux and Joues etc. I don't know quite when I shall get away. But some time in the week before Easter I hope. With what companions I do not know Crum I believe, Benson & Ryle.

We had a good performance at the ADC a week ago the "Overlaud Racte" the same piece I played in 84. The psalm of Solomon will be on the guide for Sept week.

Will write when I have more news but as I say there is too much talk for me to write.

Ever yr loving

MRJ

Notes

1. Honnington Wood was a site that was reputed to be haunted. Even in 1891 when James wrote this letter to his parents the area was surrounded by legends of ghosts, and today it is linked to the sighting of military figures that hail from the two world wars. But in James's time the hauntings were attributed to the gibbet that had been built on the hill that overlooks Honnington. There was a gallows and a gibbet there that, when unearthed, still had the remains of a convicted murderer, John Nichols (wearing the boots he had been hung in). Nichols had been accused of the murder of his daughter Sarah in spring 1794 and had been hanged for this crime, with his body displayed in the iron cage of the gibbet for everyone to see that justice had been served. The gibbet still hangs today by the door of a local museum, Moyse's Hall Museum, Bury St Edmunds.

2. The Brent Eleigh Manuscripts were seven of nine manuscripts from the parish church of Brent Eleigh in Suffolk. Two of the lot had been sold to a private collector in 1887, so time was of the essence when it came to acquiring these precious documents for either the Fitzwilliam or the university, and James had to move fast to prevent the manuscripts being left to languish in a private collection. Finding the manuscripts housed in a small dank building in the church's grounds, James started protracted negotiations, on behalf of the university. He secured the seven, which included Thomas of Monmouth's 'life' of William of Norwich, which James was later to publish with Augustus Jessop in 1896 (see Pfaff, p.99).

My Dear People

> Cambridge University Library –
> Rare Manuscripts, ADD 7480-D6-318-416,
> Letters from MRJ to his parents, 1890–1899

> Pitt Club Crest (Stamp)

> 16 March 1891

My Dear People,

I have sustained well I am glad to say. On Saturday we elected to HoD Headlam (J.W. and W.J.) to fellowship. I think it was a good election on the whole. I thought that would be the tenth or the eleventh if there are two vacancies next year.

Lionel Ford of King's ought to get in: if not Loring, but if, as I hope Lionel gets a fair number of Edwards pupils it will not much matter to him. The tutelage certainly is going to help people who are likely to want assistance and to those who do not it is a living to be made, but it helps acquaint all such people as barristers and fellows.

I helped get up here all the week before to set papers & get them printed. I go to SW France on [the 12ᵗʰ of] Wednesday week. I have happily finished the cursor papers & have not much more to do with the plays.

I see there is another Laudeman!! [Along] a boy. CW.14. I must write to congratulate later etc.

We got our £5000 for the Middle hill MSS.¹ I hope to have some voice in the selection.

> Much love
> Ever yr loving
> MRJ

Notes

1. The Middle Hill manuscripts were part of a collection that had
   been compiled by Sir Thomas Phillipps at his estate in Middle
   Hill, Worcestershire. He assembled catalogues at his private
   press on the estate to keep a track of his extensive collection,
   which amounted to some 40,000 books and 66,000 manuscripts,
   which he had started amassing while at Rugby School and later
   on at Oxford University. In 1888 James had been depressed to
   hear that Britain had missed out on acquiring the largest part of
   the collection, which instead had gone to Berlin. Later sales of
   the manuscripts were seized upon by the university (as James
   writes here) but nothing more was said about this money or why
   the Fitzwilliam did not buy any of the collection.

Dearest People

Cambridge University Library –
Rare Manuscripts, ADD 7480-D6-318-416,
Letters from MRJ to his parents, 1890–1899

Broxton Old Hall Chester (Stamp)

4 April 1891

Dearest People

We have had altogether a most successful trip.[1] We arrived in Antwerp after a calm passage on Sunday morning. Left on Monday for Mechelen. The hotel we stayed in before was fine. Left Mechelen for Louvain on Tuesday. Went to Liege on Wednesday. To Huy a very pretty place on Thursday.

Luxembourg on Friday. Triers on Saturday. Triers is lovely full of Roman buildings. Splendid Cathedral good even superlatively good during where I examined some lovely MSS. The Egbert Codex of the Gospels illustrated in 970 with 50 pictures an apocalypse of the 10th century with 74 pictures. This is what I was baptized for. I saw later at Huy leaves of a Cipher from a Roman book of about the 5th century that ushered in a fountain head for all later illustrations of the work. Also I saw what is called the Golden Book of Prum.

Prum is an Abbey nearby, Osnabruck is a 9th or 10th century: Cathedral whose tower is of copper with beautiful preludes captured on it, also an ancient MSS of 692 with the "Segur of Authentisch" an extract of an old apocalypse. At Antwerp we examined an early illustrated sardonicus 10th century at the Musee d lateau on Tuesday. We left Huys for Brussels on Friday and came Tournay I went through a sweet Psalter althea at Paternoster in Cent xiii. At Tournay we saw a splendid Cathedral & great walls of Gold Smithery with xiith century frescoes of Saint Eleutherius & St Pratt.

On Saturday we came to Ghent & late in the evening here because of a silly idea we spent a bawdy night. I shall hope to sleep at the crossing where a telegram shall be sent, and on Tuesday I hope to come to you. I have a hope of a stiff drink at the Royle at Bangor Gd Hotel de la commerce.

In the examiner at 10am to 8pm as it takes more than a day, if bad weather.

Ever yr loving

MRJ

Notes

1. See previous letter 'Dearest People', [March 1891], Pitt Club Crest. James had evidently been planning this trip to Belgium and Germany for a few months to get a well-earned break and time away: 'I can't spend the time in the necessary company to go as far as the South West of France, so I have turned my attention in other directions ...' However, not much time was spent in idle pursuits if the frantic pace of his expeditions to examine MSS and cathedrals is anything to go by. This was before he started his bicycling trips to Europe, and just before Dunlop invented the rubber tyre: according to the biography by James's friend Gurney Lubbock, 'It must be remembered that the bicycle of those days had a wheel five feet high [like the penny-farthing], on the top of which you perched precariously; and exceeding few there where who rode it,' (p.30). In fact James rode a double tandem before the invention of better cycles, and after this rode his cycle with its rubber tyres on subsequent cycling holidays.

Dearest People

Cambridge University Library –

Rare Manuscripts, ADD 7480-D6-318-416,

Letters from MRJ to his parents, 1890–1899

King's College (Stamp)

[1893]

Dearest People,

Many thanks for your: I don't know that I have much news. The chief thing to mind is that I have, I hope, cleaned up the entries to the Fitzwilliam Catalogue (there are five of them) & written a preface. Also I am expecting [to tell] the forthcoming catalogue in a bound form soon.

I don't know if I told you that R.Norman was getting on all right – settling in well and so forth. One surprise was the abdication of Dear John Henry. I don't know who will succeed him, probably Glaister or Forsyth.[1] The selection problem is also quite uncertain. I should think Prothero if he would accept it.

Some interesting MSS (early Latin) are to be sold next week in London. I shall have to go up & see them.

There is a possibility – perhaps a large one that residence will not be assured during the day vacation this year in consequence of a delaying of funds this time. I should be delighted if it were so but I fear it is too good to be true.

I have got two other communications to send off in the next ten minutes so this must do.

Probably I will go to Hertfordshire on Thursday to see an old aqt, who has some pictures. He says one of them is a Memling. He would probably give some to us.[2]

The p card history is extensor, atop a picture of St Peter's which I found at Eton a long time ago. I am going to send him, apropos of much love;

Ever yr loving

MRJ

Notes

1. John Henry Middleton resigned in 1893 to become head of the South Kensington Museum (now the Victoria and Albert Museum), an event which James refers to here rather sarcastically as Dear John Henry's 'abdication'. It was natural that James would succeed him, but in this letter he seems to think that other candidates might be preferred, demonstrating rather that it – at least in his mind – was never a concrete idea.

2. This letter although undated can be traced to 1893. This is from a perusal of the accessions register at the Fitzwilliam for 1893, which reveals the entry for the 'aqt' or 'acquaintance' in Hertfordshire who possessed the Memling. In the entry James refers to him as an 'Old Gent', whereas in this letter to his parents he terms him an acquaintance.

Dearest Pa

Cambridge University Library –
Rare Manuscripts, ADD-7480-D6 176-317,
Letters to parents 1882–1889, King's

Fitzwilliam Museum, Cambridge (Stamp)

25 October 1895

Dearest Pa

I never can remember which of your birthday dedications is the most appropriate.

However, much love & many happy returns to you. I have little that could be called news. The chief employment has been seeing Fitz manu's in the evenings. Though not a very distinguished lot, I think they are nice.[1]

It seems as if more books are coming to the Fitz. The Jesus & Eton catalogues which have never been printed off, are now in a fit state to be bound & issued, & the King's one is as well. Fourth Gaius will be out in a few days.

Some other things I have recently received at the sum tune of 30% a large book in which Haydon, his favourite one assumes, to which he used to put down his ideas for pictures. Also I have bought a book of days MS of I and II & a sketch book of Thomas Holland, & a lot of small sketches of William Hawley. Besides various images & drawings which I picked up at Radiston for very little.

Ronny Norman comes over on Wednesday for a few hours. He is extremely well & at Trinity as a reader. Starting today, he is on the look-out for a professorship.

I have priced up a lot of engraved portraits of Handel, in a drawer, at this museum.

All in a very good condition as caricatures of him as a pig playing the organ called The Charming Brute.[2]

Much love

Ever yr affect

MRJ

Notes

1. This letter was written to his father during James's tenure as director of the Fitzwilliam Museum, 1893–1908. Despite his claims that he preferred an understated approach, the record of the museum's growth and prosperity during these years demonstrates rather the opposite as its collections and finances after James's administration were considerably better off than before (see Pfaff, p.100).

2. 'The Charming Brute' is by Joseph Goupy, a close friend of Handel's, who lived nearby. However, when the two men quarrelled in 1743, Groupy drew a gouache and chalk picture of his ex-friend as a rather corpulent and satisfied pig playing his organ surrounded by the fruits of his musical successes in the form of a tableau of food and drink. The picture is still stored at the Fitzwilliam (object no.961 – paintings, drawings and prints).

My Dearest Ma

Cambridge University Library –

Rare Manuscripts, ADD 7480-D6-318-416,

Letters from MRJ to his parents, 1890–1899

King's College Crest (Stamp)

3 February 1896

My Dearest Ma,

Here is much love for your birthday. I suspect it will be a better day than today and that you will be far away from such tiresome jobs I have to do such as a syndicate meeting.

I am just at this minute writing a paper to read next week at Sion College – also making notes for my annual report to the museum. I have found a young man here who was brought up on French antiques. His name is Vulliamy – Huguenot Family no doubt.[1] He has brought his antique books here tonight. They are to be used for performing valuations for staff.

I send you a sample of tincture's of which I have heard they are good and hope they may help.

I might have to go over to Eton today for a school meeting but I've determined that there was nothing important not worth the time which I could not afford to lose.

Paul Meyer has sent me an article in which he describes me as the "sympathetique Doyen de King's College".

I received today an invitation from France & a paper which describes the acquisition & the collection in the 14th Century, of the baptism of Christ at Reims

much love

ever yr affect

MRJ

Notes

1. The origin of the word 'Huguenot' has been lost in history but its etymological root is believed to lie in the practice of home worship allowed to the Protestants in France and Germany in the sixteenth century, the first Huguenot church having been created in Paris in a private home around 1555. The Huguenots were sixteenth- and seventeenth-century French Protestants who followed the theologian John Calvin. The Huguenot name was adopted by Calvinists around 1560. However, during persecution in France by the Catholic government during the 1600s they fled to various countries, including, a small proportion to elsewhere in Europe, Ireland, Africa and America. Because of this religious flight the Huguenots are credited with bringing the word 'refugee' into the English language upon their arrival in Britain (see www.historic-uk.com/HistoryUK/HistoryofEngland /The-Huguenots for more).

My Dear Mr Cockerell[1]

British Library Archive

~~Eton College (Stamp)~~

School House, Malvern

1 October 1897

My Dear Mr Cockerell,

I am glad my letter was of some use: as to the other matter I am sorry but it is really very difficult (although I am very glad you ~~actually~~ managed) to say anything to the purpose.

I don't candidly think that there is enough work at the Fitzwilliam for two: I know that I often regarded myself as a luxury when assistant director, and that is why when I became Director I recommended the Syndicate to discontinue the office.

At the same time, if I know a purpose of getting hold of your services in some capacity at Cambridge I should jump at it. All I can do is to talk to people when I get back: and that I will do. As you know, the university is stuck for money at present and ~~[we reach to our guide what]~~ I don't myself clearly see much prospect of the kind of employment you seek but I will really do my best.

I am

Faithfully Yours

M R James

Notes

1. It is interesting to note that James's biographer Pfaff did not consult this letter, as his details about Sir Sydney Cockerell's first encounter with James are taken from the biography of Cockerell by Wilfred Blunt (1964), which Pfaff dutifully references on p.100 of his biography of James.

   Cockerell's letter to James was answered in 1897 from School House, Malvern, where James was staying with his brother Sydney who had become headmaster of Malvern College in 1897. It also appears that M. R. James was a stationery kleptomaniac as this letter was written on pilfered Eton paper with the Eton crest just casually crossed out in ink. (Although, come to think of it, the elder James brother may have been the thief as Sydney had worked as a master at Eton for some years previously!)

My Dearest Pa

Cambridge University Library –
Rare Manuscripts, ADD-7480-D6 176-317,
Letters to parents 1882–1889, King's

King's College (Stamp)

[January–February 1898]

My Dearest Pa

You want a paper or a subject. I think the paintings in East Ampton Church would be very interesting. I would want a little more time to think out the details of it. But I believe the subject could be made to work a good deal. It depends upon language and such details: but I believe it would be possible to show how it went with the development of population in the region & religion. But of this I would investigate further.

I will tell you how my days leave is going. I got to Hereford a good five miles to the Davies – a small house. The party was Lady Lyttelton who is extremely loud, Lady Caroline Lyttelton, also a very small Lyttelton, & Eustace Talbot.

On the Thursday we went to see Walter Dimsdale who lives a small way off. On Sunday early to matins. After Sunday at the BM, I went to the Porters where I helped carry the duties of ceremony at the Savoy.

Tuesday the museum again and in pantomime which fully answered all expectations.

Wednesday the college of arms, I also saw the chapel in Ely Palace. The gorgeous Roundel; of the Bishop's of Ely Palace was a RC chapel. I don't remember much else.

I went in the afternoon to the Aquarium and saw the Cinematograph of the great fight between Corbett & Fitzsimmons.[1]

Contrary to my expectations, it interested me very much, & I could not see any brutality in it.

On Thursday the National Portrait Gallery, later lunch at St Bart's with Eustace Talbot, Charterhouse in the afternoon & finished with Peter the Great at the Lyceum.

Will write more soon.

Ever yr affect

MRJ

Notes

1. The great fight between Britain's 'Bob' Fitzsimmons and the American James J. Corbett on 17 March 1897 was the world's first heavyweight boxing championship (the sport was still semi-illegal in Britain). It had been three years in the making, having been previously banned from taking place in Texas and Florida. It was ultimately fought in Carson City, Nevada for a purse of $50,000 ($1,575,795 in today's money). Taking 14 rounds, it was slugged out between the two pugilists in front of an audience of 3,000 people many of whom had paid up to £10 dollars a head to witness the spectacle. The film that James viewed at the Royal Aquarium in Westminster had used media of over two miles in length and over 165,000 stills to produce living moving pictures. After his defeat by Fitzsimmons, Corbett's look of sheer angst and his subsequent dash where he struck people in agony were depicted in absolute clarity. The Aquarium had paid production costs of £5,000 to obtain and show the film of the fight. The spectator (as James noted) was provided with a display of sportsmanship and precision, very different from the gory spectacle that may have been expected. (See picturegoing.com, 'The Great Fight at the Aquarium', The Era, 2 October 1897, p.18.)

My Dear Pa

Cambridge University Library –
Rare Manuscripts, ADD-7480-D6 176-317,
Letters to parents 1882–1889, King's

King's College (Stamp)

7 May [1898]

My Dear Pa,

I hear you are on the way. Why not arrive here for Sunday? You will be here for the talk: you shall sleep in my room, whence a short walk at the back of the college is easy without going out of doors.

You will be with me and Walter Durnford & further companions & so on & intellectual talk & what not & victuals will be had. I have no further particular work then. I had a dinner planned for Friday night but I have explained to the Lady host that I shall be prevented from attending that.

I hear with anxiety that R.Norman has suffered a relapse, but I remain optimistic.

McBryde is through his examinations and continues at St Bartholomew's with a light heart.[1]

Much love everybody
MRJ

Notes

1. James McBryde is often a controversial character to those who
   have written anything of a biographical nature on James. Some
   see him as a very close friend, some view him as the great love of
   James's life. But the nature of MRJ's feeling for him is indicated
   in a draft of a letter written on his behalf to a comparative
   stranger in (probably) 1902: 'I have no younger brother and he
   rather takes the place of one in my life' (Pfaff, p.110). There is no
   evidence of anything other than friendship between the two
   men. However, James's behaviour after McBryde's death (from
   complications arising from an operation for a burst appendix on
   9 June 1904) rather throws open more questions than answers.
   Cox outlines this: 'Monty travelled up to Lancashire [where the
   funeral was being held] by train with Walter Fletcher, taking
   with him roses, syringa and honeysuckle from the Fellow's
   Garden at King's.' However, James then waited until the very
   last mourner had departed and then threw the flowers into the
   grave (p.128). This is not so much the behaviour of just a friend,
   but really rather more romantic in its semantic markers, of
   flowers, mourning and loss. The Victorians believed in using the
   symbolism of flowers to spell out messages, so if we look at the
   markers inherent in this selection, honeysuckle stands for true
   love, syringa for first love and roses for love (depending on their
   colour: white for purity and innocence, red for romantic love).
   All in all there is much to wonder about here.

My Dear Family

Cambridge University Library –
Rare Manuscripts, ADD-7480-D6 176-317,
Letters to parents 1882–1889, King's

King's College (Stamp)

[March 1899]

My Dear Family[1]

There is not a great deal to report. The Lent boat races have begun, & I am always relieved when the evening after them is over because visitors at the ferry area are apt to be going when all is done, then I can get to bed about 1.30am.

Many days have been spent over the Fitzwilliam accounts. For a long time they were 5/6 awry and yesterday they had really changed with about £15 out and then they came right. Its extraordinary what numbers will do if you add them up a few times.

Nixon is talking again about chapel service numbers and I daresay that we are going to meet him half the way.

Noting events lately. I am in the middle of nasty paper work at Trinity – which yields very little satisfaction.

I had a very pleasant bicycle ride last week – the first this term - on one of the really good days, with Marcus Dimsdale and Percy Lubbock. The latter is much more proficient than Marcus but I think he enjoys himself.

Next week I have Walter Morley Fletcher for a few days as he has to go to town to receive a typhoid vaccination in hospital. I had planned to go to Bayreuth with him next August to hear the Wagner – but all my efforts were alas in vain as there are no bicycles to be had, and quite an effort to get them in time to be able to get to the continent. I'm afraid it was not to be.

Much love to
everybody
yr affect
MRJ

Notes

1. The family unit had changed much since the death of Mary Emily, James's mother, at age 80 at Livermere in September 1898. His brother Sydney (who had been a house master at Eton since James's senior year there) had successfully applied for the headmaster's position at Malvern College, and was married in April 1897 to Linda Hoare, whose uncle owned Ampton Hall, half a mile from the James family home of Livermere. On the strength of this success he had also been ordained a priest, having been a deacon since 1883. This letter would have been read by just the two of the James clan present in Livermere at the time: Herbert, James's father, and his sister Grace, who was still living at the family home at the age of 39.

My Dear People

Cambridge University Library –
Rare Manuscripts, ADD-7480-D6 176-317,
Letters to parents 1882–1889, King's

King's College (Stamp)

[May 1899]

My Dear People,

It is long indeed since we exchanged letters. I have a picture of St Bertrand De Comminges for Gracy which should have made me write before.[1] On May 1st I went to Ely for a school meeting: and on the way back stopped at the locks for two hours and a quarter. The water there was a little off the lane at six inches at the bottom.

R. Norman stayed with me last Sunday & I hope McB will come for the next one.

A sale of MSS is on the way, I examined a very nice XIIth Century Bestiary for the Fitzwilliam with lots of pictures of animals.

Robinson wrote today to get me to go up with his Dean & tender my opinion on a large cross which lord Rosebay intends to present to the abbey. I think I will go on Monday.

I spend my days tranquilly with MSS – Alwyne Compton has brought me a Psalter that belonged to Carrow Priory at Norwich & has an Oyster Bosses series of pictures, which I have just got the key to.[2] They represent only half and I am planning to do MSS (seriously) at there and at Christ's: I have made overtures to Clare.

I expect daily to see Peterhouse.[3] I have indicated to Broadbent Robinson's discovery has shed insight as in-sighting you.

Much love

Ever yr loving

MRJ

Notes

1. Saint-Bertrand-De-Comminges is a southern French town in which James set his famous ghost story 'Canon Alberic's Scrapbook'.

2. James made the acquaintance of Lord Alwyne Compton, Bishop of Ely, through his work on deciphering why the statues at the Lady Chapel at Ely were broken. This discovery was made by the Fitzwilliam's acquisition of a book on the Carew-Poyntz Hours: a fourteenth-century book of hours, full of pictures of the depictions of the Virgin – among them illustrations which showed how the statues would have looked before they were desecrated. (See James, *Eton and King's*, pp.207–8.)

3. James had long harboured 'a cherished design' to make catalogues of all the manuscripts held in the Cambridge colleges. Obviously King's was the first college that he started this large undertaking with, followed by Sidney Sussex in Lent term 1893 and Jesus College in spring 1893: other colleges followed on. For a full description of the process, see Pfaff, pp.172–208.

Dearest Pa

Cambridge University Library –
Rare Manuscripts, ADD-7480-D6 176-317,
Letters to parents 1882–1889, King's

King's College (Stamp)

[May–June 1898]

Dearest Pa,

I don't quite know which day if any this week will serve. Tomorrow we have Christies Valuations, Friday is most likely, Saturday we have meetings.

My two other days are no better: this rather sums up Corpus and I hope to complete them: also I hope Adam Fruit.[1]

I am dreadful busy & I have just discovered this morn that I have three lectures on non canonical revelations to deliver before June 22nd, when I travel to deliver them at Leeds.

And then. And then, there are just forty thousand other things like the Tripos: and I am dining again at Lambeth & looking at their stuff. Well I suppose there is no rest for the wicked.

I have a new book to read & lecture upon a thick work by Dr Butler, by Saturday on Palladius Historia Lausiaca and the Trinity MSS are particularly fascinating.

In hurry to do many other things.

Much love
Ever yr affect
MRJ

Notes

1. James was working on various manuscript collections at the time of writing this letter to his father. The collection in Corpus Christi College was one that he did have trouble with, as even now there are references to 'James's incomplete catalogue' (see jstor.org). The reference to 'Adam Fruit' here seems an obscure one even for James, until some research turns up the references to the Rood Legend which is part of the manuscripts in the Corpus library. This is a whole area of study, encompassing the Apocryphal texts of the Bible (Old and New testament), medieval English literature and the Old English poem 'The Dream of the Rood', which Dr Patrick J. Murphy has shown was a particular obsession of James's and can be found referenced in many of his ghost stories, including 'The Stalls of Barchester Cathedral' and 'An Evening's Entertainment' (see Murphy, index).

My Dearest People

Cambridge University Library –
Rare Manuscripts, ADD 7480-D6-318-416,
Letters from MRJ to his parents, 1890–1899

King's College (Stamp)

[Summer 1899]

My Dearest People,

I have been working away diligently this last week and have little to no news. I think I may be going to Bury in 2 weeks to lecture on some chapels there.

I have nearly finished one supplement register of the Trinity MSS – nearly 400 and if there were not about 500 other things to be done in the next week I would be really pleased.[1]

I have turned up another of T.Becket's works, and also what I think is an autograph of an hortis conclusus a poem that he gave to Canterbury.

I have also finished writing out a great catalogue of folios in English, dry work usually but which is a delight with my old favourite Bosworth of Bunny's which is still extant, but whether it is in earlier or later is not yet clear.[2]

I have been over to two archival expeditions on the bicycle – to St Eds last night and to Rutherford the night before. If it were fine weather I want to go to Ashwell.

McBryde has stated his intention of coming over to King's for a night. I hope he may.

Much love
Yr affect
MRJ

Notes

1. The Trinity MSS is described by James's biographer Richard Pfaff as 'the masterpiece' among the early manuscripts that James catalogued. The pages he had transcribed and catalogued numbered over 1,500; it had made him very nervous as an academic undertaking owing to the size and variety of the manuscripts. It was a challenge much larger than the previous collections of King's and Peterhouse, and all of the other colleges combined, and was the work of over five years (Pfaff, p.186).

    For an overview of James's views on paleography, philology and cataloguing manuscripts see his pamphlet on this subject, *The Wanderings and Homes of Manuscripts* (London: Society for Promoting Christian Knowledge; New York: Macmillan, 1919).

2. James refers to 'Bosworth of Bunny's' as his favourite work for translating Old English. The work is known nowadays as the Bosworth Toller dictionary. Bosworth was born in Derbyshire in 1788, and initially gained enough knowledge to be trained as a priest by the Church of England. He then became a curate in Bunny, Nottinghamshire (hence Bosworth of Bunny's), and held a special interest in Anglo-Saxon language, which led to him compiling the first major Anglo-Saxon dictionary in 1823, and matriculating at Trinity College Cambridge later that same year. (See ebeowulf.uky.edu/BT/Bosworth-Toller.htm for a history and background on Bosworth, and the later scholars who worked on this dictionary.)

We have arrived safely

Rev H James
Livermere Rectory
Bury St Edmunds
England

1 July 1899

Postcard from M. R. James to Herbert James from Brekfort, Sweden

We have arrived safely here & have just been breakfasting in the Inn – superb (praktig) with the Vice-Provost & his Fiancée Miss Whiting. We propose to sally forth soon & see the 14 churches. Will write again – letter – I don't know where but are planning for last leg to get to Luxembourg next.[1]

Much love
MRJ

Notes

1. James had long held an interest in Sweden. His friend Stephen Gaselee wrote in his memoirs that James had learned Swedish on many of their long European train journeys in order to be able to translate Nordic folktales and stories from their original language. There was much speculation as to where this interest was first kindled for James. He noted in his letters home to his parents when at his preparatory school, that he wanted to learn more about 'Leprechauns' and other fairies, but it may have been the under-librarian at Cambridge University Library when James was an undergraduate, Erikur Magnusson, an Icelander, who inspired this love of Nordic folklore. Certainly, he was very well versed in this area and specifically Scandinavian fairy tales.

This interest found further fertile ground when in 1924 James agreed to collaborate on a small volume of translations of Hans Christian Andersen's tales with Arthur Benson, but after Benson's death in 1927, James abandoned this project until the spring of 1927, when he began the arduous task of translating the texts into English. In the following year he gave two speeches, one at Cambridge and another at Eton, on Andersen. By late 1928 most of the 40 stories had been translated into English.

James's ghost stories have two specific settings in a Scandinavian country: 'No.13', which is set in Denmark, and 'Count Magnus', set in Sweden. However, his travels across Scandinavia certainly provided the inspiration not just for his ghost stories, but also for the inclusion of folklore in the stories and his full-length children's fairy-tale novel, *The Five Jars*, as well as his translation of Hans Christian Andersen.

My Dearest Pa

Cambridge University Library –
Rare Manuscripts, ADD 7480-D6-318-416,
Letters from MRJ to his parents, 1890–1899

King's College (Stamp)

26 October [1899]

My Dearest Pa,

So glad to hear of you. I wanted to send a line for the 28th but was unsure of where the Bernard's lived & where you were.[1] All life to you & much love – away the archdi for the cutting. Grant and I drank your health at Hall just now.

I met Flinders Petrie yesterday, both in appearance & in manner he seems to me very Arabian.[2]

I think you know most of us or have met most or at least can judge of what sort they are likely to be. [I see that old Carter was over] We brought a Lus Chromide from St Augustine's Canterbury, for the dining hall yesterday: and within the last few days I have been hearing of a good way to get a list of St Augustine's books.[3]

Also we talk of old Beaky Carter's projected resignation, after Eton, professorship. He is a very good prospect anyway.

Much love
Evr yr affect

Notes

1. At this point in James's life much had changed with his family
   unit at home (see letter 'My Dear Family', [March 1899], King's).
   As mentioned in the context to that letter, after James's mother
   Mary Emily's death, Sydney had married: then in his seventy-
   seventh year Herbert James appointed a curate, Revd John
   Edward Woodhouse, whom Grace was to marry ten years after
   Herbert's death. With a curate at the rectory, Herbert was at
   long last able to get out and about as he wished. This letter from
   James finds him visiting the home of the Bernards, and for the
   first time James was not sure exactly of his father's whereabouts
   rather than vice-versa (which, come to think of it, might have
   pleased the elder James, now delighting in the freedom of his
   second childhood it seems). Herbert regularly visited his son
   at the rooms that he had occupied since 1893, in the Wilkins
   Building at King's. In his initial occupation he had new curtains,
   carpets and bookcases fitted, and hired a piano.

2. Flinders Petrie was Sir William Matthew Flinders Petrie,
   nicknamed 'Flinders', an English Egyptologist and a pioneer of
   systematic methodology in archaeology and the preservation of
   artefacts. He was the holder of the first chair in Egyptology in
   the United Kingdom, at University College London, and in his
   long career excavated many of the most important archaeological
   sites in Egypt, including Abydos, the Giza Plateau and that of
   the Merneptah Stele. One of his trainees, Howard Carter, went
   on to discover the tomb of the supposedly cursed Tutankhamun
   in 1922. Petrie developed the system of dating layers based on
   pottery and ceramic fragments excavated at the digs he
   supervised. One can only imagine the conversation between
   James and Petrie.

3. James was very interested in trying to catalogue the books and
   manuscripts at St Augustine's, particulary those of the tenth

century or thereabouts. He turned up at this time 'Two Volumes
of Juvenal from St Augustine's' and 'A Rule of St Benedict',
which Pfaff states he wrongly dated to the ninth century, rather
than the tenth century (see Pfaff, p.190, for a fuller explanation of
all of the manuscripts James uncovered).

My Dearest Pa

Cambridge University Library –
Rare Manuscripts, ADD 7480-D6-318-416,
Letters from MRJ to his parents, 1890–1899

King's College (Stamp)

[November–December 1899]

My Dearest Pa,

Cooke has been made headmaster of Aldenham so the sel[ection]
is – where I said it would be – in the air. It seems [at] rather probable
that I may become tutor.[1]

There are many imagined appointees, one week its Cooke & then
O.B. & O Purcell & next V.J. I should of course be immensely
relieved if McCauley say were made tutor instead but if I am asked,
I must not say no. It would be an intricate trade to learn but I hope
possible: and it would entail my laying aside in great part the jobs I
am interested in. But I have signified to the provost that if appointed
I should wish to leave off being Dean as soon as possible and that I
should not wish to give up the museum.

It would be advisable I think to pull in an assistant Director – these
and any ideas could be put to use as part of the Director job for this
period & thereafter. But the tutorship won't be given again and to be
given the part really with little difficulties: but also I will have left
everything in excellent order, & I should wish to carry on the trade [in]
not in my own rooms but in the place where it will be awarded.

I believe the tutorship is likely to be offered on Sunday.

Much love
Ever yr affect

Notes

1. James had enjoyed being a dean at King's but tradition dictated that he could not continue holding this position into his forties. Then the present tutor A. H. Cooke took up the position of headmaster at Aldenham School, and a selection process – and the inevitable rumour mill in as small a world as King's – started.

James was appointed to the role after the process and found himself in a position that had become one of real power and influence as, since reforms in the 1880s and from 1892, there was now only one tutor, who was in effect the director of studies for every undergraduate in the college, and responsible for the administration of new undergraduates.

James gave up many of the jobs that he had enjoyed, including the deanship, and lightened his load at the Fitzwilliam Museum by arranging (as he suggested in this letter) for an assistant director to help with the more routine day-to-day jobs. The onslaught of administrative duties then commenced: councils, scholarships, meetings, library selections, and at the end of October 1900 he also found himself having to act as general tutor to the classical first years at King's.

This round of duties was unsurprisingly anathema to someone as focused on his own research as James and he talked then of resigning (as we will see in letters to come), even though he had only been in the job 11 months. However, the reason for his selection in the first place was that he had been viewed as being part of what came to be seen at King's as 'The Godly Party', in that he was not an avowed atheist. Any other selection would not fit in with the changing scene at what was a very traditional institution. Under these conditions James (for now) gave way and stayed in post.

My Dear Pa

Cambridge University Library –
Rare Manuscripts, ADD 7480-D6-417-561,
Letters from James to his Father & Grace,
1900–1906, King's

King's College (Stamp)

[January 1900]

My Dear Pa,

They have indeed made me a Tutor today – quod bene vortat – I do not propose as at present advised to lecture nor to continue to be Dean. On the other duties I do propose to stop at the Fitzwilliam & probably to get leave to appoint an Assistant Director.[1] The new trade will take some time to master. At the moment I have no time to make more.

Much love
Ever yr affec
MRJ

Notes

1. Strangely not everyone in James's life was ecstatic at the news of him becoming tutor. His old tutor (always given the title even in adult life as M'Tutor) H. E. Luxmoore sounded a note of caution as Cox noted:

> He was doubtful if the appointment was a wise one either for King's or for Monty.
>
> Of course it's a compliment to elect him and shews due honour from his College ... But either it might stir him up out of his somewhat unproductive groove, for he does 'produce' too little for his powers! Or it might just take him from what suits him to more office work, which he might not exert himself enough to fulfil. One can't fancy him writing letters, and while he exercises the old charm on his old circle he may fail to exert himself to reach the less congenial undergraduates. It is a doubtful prospect!

A doubtful prospect indeed. Straight away upon his appointment, as Luxmoore had predicted, James was thrust into an uncongenial whirl of administrative duties, from overseeing admissions to hiring rooms, and it was not long before James felt overburdened and began to look for a way out.

Dear Mr Cockerell

British Library Archive

King's College (Stamp)

3 May 1900

Dear Mr Cockerell,

Many thanks: I will note the existence of Lord Crawford's MSS of Biography. I have never read it.[1]

I am surprised at Delisle the most I would concede is that five of these apocalypses may be Anglo-Norman.[2] But even the Paris one has certainly been in England.

There is a xvith cent incantation in it of which I Know the hand – only I cannot yet remember whose it is.

The St Genevieve marble I only know as a set by reputation: & I have no idea which of the Canterbury prebendaryies it came from.[3] I have never even seen a full copy of its inscription.

Could you tell me anything about your Canterbury Bible at the Bib. Nat. I should like to know if it is a St Augustine's or a Christ Church book.

Not that I know anything of this St Augustine at the Laurentian Library.

I am just pre-pressing [beginning to print] a bit of the Lambeth MSS with bib Cambridge I suppose the Psalter no. 233 is ready anytime?

Do you know the annotation in it?

I am very truly

M R James

Notes

1. When at the Fitzwilliam Museum James had noted that he was at a disadvantage when it came to cataloguing items such as coins and stamps, but as this letter to Sydney Cockerell demonstrates, their relationship had the advantages of Cockerell's knowledge in the areas where James's was lacking. The recommendation of the MSS written by Lord Crawford was a good one as it contained an explanation of rare coins and stamps (never it seems an interest of James's).

2. The classifications of the apocalypses referred to by Cockerell here are from a classification by Léopold Delisle. Manchester University Library locates the manuscripts in the John Rylands Library and identifies this manuscript as being from the first third of the fourteenth century in (as indeed James identified it) northern France. It is comprised of pictures only, and inscribed with the accompanying legends underneath the accompanying text from the university library notes:

> This is one of four manuscripts which constitute the 'first family' of illustrated Apocalypses in M. Delisle's classification: the other three being (1) MS. Fr. 403, Paris Bibl. Nat.; (2) Bodley Auct. D. 4. 17, reproduced by H. O. Coxe for the Roxburghe Club in 1876; (3) a manuscript owned by M. le Vicomte Blin de Bourdon, of which two pages are reproduced by MM. Delisle and Meyer as plates ii and iii of the appendix to their reproduction of the Paris MS. Fr. 403. This first family is distinguished from others by its inclusion of a series of subjects from the life of St. John at the beginning and end of the Apocalypse, and of two pictures illustrating the miracles and triumphs of Antichrist. The resemblance between our manuscript and that in the Bodleian extends, as M. Delisle says, to the most minute

details, e. g. the armorial bearings emblazoned on flags, shields, etc. The number of figures in the groups is uniformly identical in both. The chief differences appear in the treatment of armour and of architecture: in these two respects the artist has introduced the styles of his own day. Pale purples, reds, and greens are the prevailing colours: faces are softly drawn and stippled. The grounds are left plain throughout. (See: www.digitalcollections. manchester.ac.uk/view/MS-LATIN-00019/1 – accessed on 12 May 2021)

3. The letter also shows that James was still engaged in identifying the marble statues at Canterbury Cathedral, and St Genevieve had been suggested as one of the likenesses. It is not stated whether anything came of this research. St Genevieve is the patron saint of Paris, and as such her statue can be found in the Luxembourg Gardens after being commissioned from Michel Mercier and placed there by Louis Phillippe I, having been completed relatively recently in James's time (1845).

My Dearest Pa

Cambridge University Library –
Rare Manuscripts, ADD 7480-D6-417-561,
Letters from James to his Father & Grace,
1900–1906, King's

King's College (Stamp)

[October 1900]

My Dearest Pa,

Still a dearth of news: usual preparations for the term. An entrance examination with a few candidates I expect our total will be about 45, another ten I hope. A good many of the freshmen are up already for little go and what not. They seem a very decent lot, though it is early days yet to say which of these is going to be of interest.

In the intervals of administration I have been handling papers for the antiquarian society on such interesting subjects as the paintings formerly in the chapter house at Worcester: a painting of the revolt of the Macabee's, also there: & the sculptures on the South Portal of Malmesbury Abbey.[1] The whole set of paintings are only known by cipher of late, names which are inscribed on them. However, I found one set in an MS at Worcester, the other in a MS at Clare.

I think that if I can get over to Leicester any time soon, I must do so. There are sculptures there which want correct descriptions C. R. Cockerell wrote a book about the statues at Wells (which I have) & appended with another list of various sculptures at other Cathedrals: among them the angel choir at Lincoln – terrible monument it is: but as they are the best Xiiith century depiction we have I should like to see if anything else pertinent can be made of them. But I shan't possibly be able to get over to you or elsewhere just yet.

I shall be acting as assistant curator to the classical foundation this term: it does not imply solidarity with them but telling them I shall instead, chiefly also I shall be marking various examination papers & essays.

I hope you will hold for me as you ought are there any books you would like, light or heavy? I have just discovered that the term I'm after – tot in yvetot *sic* & other such Huguenot names is the same as toft *sic*.

Much love
Ever yr loving
MRJ

Notes

1. These small-scale antiquarian investigations were quite fruitful for James, in particular the society papers on the sculptures of the south portal of Malmesbury Abbey and on the west front at Lincoln Cathedral, on which James read papers (13 March 1901, along with a paper on the Canterbury windows). At Malmesbury, the figures were already crumbling when James wrote his paper. The archaeologist and architect C. R. Cockerell had inaccurately described them in his book as being part of an agricultural plan involving the monthly signs of the zodiac and it had aroused James's ire. James re-identified them as being part of a biblical cycle, which included that of the Psychomachia by Prudentius, especially the figures in the outermost cordon of the Malmesbury figures; this gave him a much surer platform from which to operate than Cockerell's. He also correctly dated the west front sculptures at Lincoln to the early eleventh century, arguing that 'They were not designed to occupy their present position; and a little closer inspection will shew that the order in which they are arranged cannot possibly be correct' (Pfaff, p.135).

My Dear Pa

> Cambridge University Library –
> Rare Manuscripts, ADD 7480-D6-417-561,
> Letters from James to his Father & Grace,
> 1900–1906, King's
>
> King's College (Stamp)
>
> 11 February 1901

My Dear Pa,

I don't think I have any striking thoughts today, never mind this week. We had a couple of busy weekdays & on Saturday in which we served on a step in the altar of chapel = deciding definitely to order an altar.

Further McBryde came up on Thursday. He has got further examinations at his London hospital & is very cheerful. I need hardly say that he asked after you. The rest of the week seems to be featureless: to put words in the affections is the betrayal of himself: that is another way of saying that I aught probably to have been doing something else.

The second volume is really very nearly ready: I shall be delighted if I have made a clean job of that. But no.3 will take me a long time. But of course: I cannot make news when there is none.

I hope you think Latham's book clever & good. I must say I think he has got hold of a very good idea about the grave digger.

> Much love
> Ever yr affec
> MRJ

My Dear People

23 April 1901[1]

My Dear People,

I came back from Albi on Sunday I believe. I have covered much ground in a short space of time since then.

Monday morning I spent in the town library copying a piece of early MS at 1.37 we left the place & travelled on the mufti in comfort apace to Pau via Limoges through a tract of country which begins to be familiar almost.

Pau at 4.30 next morning after some breakfast in bed I went to find J.M. (late to my appointment) I went with him to the Bibliotheteque Nationale to be introduced to one of his friends there & then to the Bibl: Ste Genevieve to see a Bible of the Xiith century & a Canterbury Suite also we looked in at a good many churches & most excellent shops just had gone on by the day train by myself: the other boys were larking about in pairs.[2]

We met again in the evening & took the night train to Dover with the old predicaments of a lavage for it had been raining heavily & thundering in Paris. We were deceived & I folded my jacket & went to sleep. Owen Smith went straight on to town, Johnny Maxwell & I went for a half at the at the Lord Warden & reached Canterbury by lunch & spent a very interesting 3 or 4 hours there. We only went to the Cathedral & St Augustine's & left it at something after 4 & went to M's house in Belgrave Square where I saw only his Aunt Lady Susan Maxwell. Owen S came to dinner & the Earl Grey was sent out for but not on time.

It's a beautiful house but J.M. lives at no.48 all the Spanish pictures are there. I bade him farewell next morning. I went to the British Museum until 4 o' clock, looking at MSS particularly those which J.O.Halliwell stole in 1841 from the Trinity Library.[3]

I came on here therefore by some time on Thursday & have reacquainted with the groove spending these magnificent Summer afternoons most exclusively in Trinity & Kings. At present McB is here for an examination I trust he may get through this time. He is in the penultimate year of his medical career & the one after this is much easier. He wishes his remembrances to you.

I certainly must bet on this time as one of the best of Julys to be had in this island & Maxwell's company added very much to it. He is always up to the walks & very keen on everything he sees & never cross. I went to see him at Penicuik, with an eye to the Glasgow MSS. I found a pile of letters on my return, nothing very agitating. I shan't catch the post before I close this up.

Much love

Ever yr affec

MRJ

The central tooth has disappeared: they have such hard crusts in France.

Notes

1. Marked as [23.04.1901] in the UL records but in actuality in the letter James is clearly writing about July.
2. Strangely as a figure who was so important to James, Johnny Maxwell is not mentioned in any of James's biographies, or in his own autobiography. His omission in itself raises questions for any researcher in Jamesian studies.
3. J. O. Halliwell was, as Pfaff terms him, 'a notable scoundrel' (p.324). He was the son-in-law of Sir Thomas Phillipps, a distinguished collector of manuscripts and art. Pfaff quotes James writing about the Trinity manuscripts in class O, in the time that he was cataloguing them: 'The fate of all of these was the same; as MRJ wrote of the defective one, "*they came into the hands* [italics his] of J. O. Halliwell, who sold them to Rodd, from whom they were purchased by the British Museum" around 1840' (Pfaff, p.190). Pfaff then notes that he felt James was circumspect in passing over this theft so quickly. However, it would seem from this letter that Halliwell's activities had piqued his interest, and in his own quiet way, he was looking into the thefts. Indeed, James would encounter more work with Halliwell later on, in the cataloguing of the effects of the Elizabethan mage and occultist John Dee's papers.

Dear Pa

Cambridge University Library –
Rare Manuscripts, ADD 7480-D6-417-561,
Letters from James to his Father & Grace,
1900–1906, King's

King's College (Stamp)

30 September 1901

Dear Pa,

I am glad you like the books. I have very little news to give of myself. On Sunday in furtherance of a telegram I went to the Library in Bury & spent the afternoon pouring over the MSS which are an interesting lot: they have just 100 there are more from St Martin's Priory than anywhere else one or two from Norwich one from Malvern one from Bury.[1] The St Martin's I must trace definitely. I must see the other copy in the Brit Museum before I can even arrive at a possible date.

On Thursday I visited the James clan in the way of a diversion.[2] There were two Mrs Hollewashers, 1 Miss Lawley, 1 elderly Miss Halliwell, Sister of Lady T. I didn't see Lord T who is better.

On Saturday I walked across to Shrublands & took my lunch there with them. The blessed Lady was away as was Janie. James was absorbed in a sketch to the De Saumarez children & that continued to amuse them altogether I was well pleased that I had gone there.

Reluctantly I am planning to turn in now. There will be news tomorrow.

Much love
Ever yr affect
MRJ

Notes

1. The Bury manuscripts were a lifetime's work for James. Although ostensibly begun when he was a schoolboy, he returned to them over and over in the course of his academic career. Pfaff put forth the idea that James's work on the Bury manuscripts arose from his fascination with 'the bibliographical investigations of a fourteenth- century cataloguer' (p.200), the writer of the *Catalogus Scriptorum Ecclesiae*, who James thought was in fact one John Boston. His work on this was never published, which is why we find him still at work on this particular subject at this point in 1901.

2. Shrublands was the home of James's cousin Janie (Lady de Saumarez), in Suffolk. He often visited here and also used it as a base from which to cycle over to visit various spots to view antiquities.

My Dear Pa

Cambridge University Library –
Rare Manuscripts, ADD 7480-D6-417-561,
Letters from James to his Father & Grace,
1900–1906, King's

King's College (Stamp)

26 April [1902]

My Dear Pa,

I am very sorry to hear from G that you are in a state of petite santé again; but glad that you seem on the mend.

The beginning of term has run its accelerated course the medical incidents number 15, all years have had all examinations & are leaving next week to finish it.

Eustace Talbot has returned from Davos. I saw him today & believe he is taller than ever: he seems very well.

Ronny Norman I grieve to hear has had another operation.

Walter Durnford has been having a nasty attack of gout.

O.B. is back – same as ever. I wish he had got a lucrative appointment in Bedlam.[1]

Today I have been in meetings most of the time. Mid-afternoon I went to a house in the town to look at some pictures: two of the paintings I saw were particularly good: one may be a Velasquez. Wish I could think that we could get it for the Fitzwilliam.

The early part of last week was spent in copying out the text of Plato's Charmides only translated in the XVI century it occupies one hundred odd folio pages & will take a lot of time: but it is the only way to get a text one can use.[2] I shall divide it into paragraphs and emend it. You will see a short account of it by me in the Bradford Church Cryer.

I think it futile (& my opinions given) that the Fitzwilliam Syndicate will think it undeniable that I should continue here to be tutor.[3] Anyhow I shall have to ask that their precise date, for My appointment now has to end at Michaelmas; and I know that I should like them to answer it. I have my assistant Director to answer their queries & I know of no-one to replace him. It will be a relief to get rid of it.

Much love

Ever yr affect

MRJ

Notes

1. Oscar Browning, that perennial thorn in James's side, was back at Cambridge at this point in James's life. Both Pfaff and Cox give an account of the two men's relationship throughout their long years of knowing each other, but it is Cox perhaps who gives the best account of what seems like a simple clash of personalities:

> Monty never wholly conquered his early dislike of him, although he conceded that his abilities 'sometimes reminded one of genius'. He continued to deplore Browning's egoism, his belligerence towards Eton, and his volatility; for his part Browning criticized Monty's blind loyalty to Eton, which he felt hindered King's from stepping boldly into an independent future. (p.162)

The two were, however, destined to always be in each other's academic orbit throughout their long lives and careers.

2. Plato's 'Charmides' is a dialogue in which Socrates engages a youth named Charmides in a discussion about philosophy in which various topics are debated, such as what the Greek idea of sophrosyne or 'temperance' actually means as a practice in everyday life. The meaning could be translated ultimately as 'knowing thyself' but even this is eventually seen within the discussion as unsatisfactory. Altogether the text functions as a tool to teach the practice of debate, particularly in the way that James proposed to use it in academic debate.

3. As noted here James gave up the tutorship at the instigation of the Fitzwilliam syndics, but he was never totally satisfied in his appointment as tutor. Although he viewed it as an honour, the administration and duties that the post required did seem to weigh more heavily on him than he liked (see previous letters for context on the appointment), and as his old school tutor Luxmoore had predicted, James did not hold the appointment for long.

My Dear People

Cambridge University Library –
Rare Manuscripts, ADD 7480-D6-417-561,
Letters from James to his Father & Grace,
1900–1906, King's

King's College (Stamp)

[August 1902]

My Dear People,

Many thanks for all letters. I spent some time home Saturday to Thursday then to Wales for a week then home again til about the 24th. Then off to Scotland then home again. I leave again because staying here as the Cambridge August Matches are on the way which we are avoiding.

On about last Friday I went to a dig in Thanet in Essex.

At the moment there is an orgy going on in Hall the servants' annual match is being followed by its annual supper: I have escaped & have been feeding in my rooms, Lubbock, Hawksay and Scho.[1]

As usual I have left off my work & rue the day: but I have made a good dent in the Trinity MSS.[2]

Much love
Ever yr loving
MRJ

Notes

1. Alwyn Schofield was a new friend made at this point in James's life. He was an Old Etonian who arrived at King's College in 1903: he was a bibliophile, and very prominent in the area of drama in the college. Known as Scho, he remained a close friend to James for the rest of his life.

2. The Trinity MSS that kept James occupied during this long summer was the third volume, which appeared in published form in late autumn 1902. The collection included works given to Trinity by Roger Gale, the son of the seventeenth-century antiquarian Thomas Gale, and included works of (as James noted) 'a most pleasingly miscellaneous character'.

   The miscellaneous items included books from the libraries of Patrick Young, the librarian of the early Stuarts, and scientific and astrological works by a character who was always of interest, Dr John Dee.

My Dear Pa

Cambridge University Library –
Rare Manuscripts, ADD 7480-D6-417-561,
Letters from James to his Father & Grace,
1900–1906, King's

King's College (Stamp)

[Michaelmas 1902]

My Dear Pa,

I hear at the present that you have been obliged to take to bed for a day or two? I hope you will obey as you should.

I must see if there are any respectable diversions to amuse you.

There have not been many developments since your visit. I have had some few visitors, Yates-Thompson turned up today, and later on one P.Grenfell who is soon going to marry a Miss Howarth en seconds noces I hope she will look after him – properly.

McBryde has got through his latest Cambridge exam & only has the last exam to think of.

Syndicates are frequent. I have one on Tuesday at which Ridgeway & J.W. Clark will meet. I trust there will be no painful scenes but J.W. threatens to say the most dreadful things.

I have got my rubbings of the brass of St Henry from Finland.[1] It is a magnificent thing: besides the full length effigy of this saint it has almost a dozen taken from his life and plates describing the sides of the altar & the rest of the set.

I have had too much to do for too many people recently to allow me any time to get on with my own work: I really must find means to get more to myself.

I must now turn in for the night & mind you take care of yourself.

Much love

Ever yr affect

MRJ

Notes

1. James had read of St Henry of Finland in a six-volume history
   of Sweden (Swedish being one of the many languages he was
   proficient in) and had contacted the Finnish art historian J. J.
   Tikkanen to procure the sets of rubbings mentioned here. One
   he placed in the Fitzwilliam, another in the South Kensington
   Museum. The rubbings delineate in detail the slab top brass of
   St Henry in pontifical vestments, 13 panels around the sides of
   which tell of his deeds in Finland and his martyrdom in around
   1158. James found these brass plates to be unique, pronouncing
   them 'an adaptation of the custom of representing the lives of
   saints on the sides of the metal shrines containing their relics'
   (Pfaff, p.134).

My Dear Pa

Cambridge University Library –

Rare Manuscripts, ADD 7480-D6-417-561,

Letters from James to his Father & Grace,

1900–1906, King's

King's College (Stamp)

25 April [1903]

My Dear Pa,

We managed our journey home very well. With a good arrival from France to Southampton, & with great pleasure I took a bath and then took lunch with SM in town, & settled matters that Lubbock & his wife should pay me a visit on the 8th.

I came here on the Tuesday afternoon therefore & found letters waiting from you for which much thanks. I don't know what to say of Bury's centrepiece or trusting Albert Lawson with other news; and I can't tell him anything about the skull, for the information is the property of the Suffolk Archaeological society until unearthed I suppose.[1]

I have entangled myself lately in curating Tomlins old revision of Jocelin De Brakelond for Sir E. Clarke who is bringing out a new edition of it: I only found 17 pages in over 200 which did not require correction.[2]

The work of syndicates has already begun: however Monday I spent all day with the master of Trinity over this Westminster Reading Prize. Tuesday aught to see me at Eton, not for the night I think if I can manage to finish it. I [must see if] have to suffer the committee of Camb on the memorial. On Wednesday I have the little matter of this chapel here. I do not know when I shall get to write the various lectures & MSS which await me. I have 35 then all of the Caius & Emmanuel etc etc. But I daresay it will right itself. However, in the meantime this weather now will be taking a warmer turn. We said we will return to France which we could in summer.

The Gaelic language still occupies me mildly although I should like to acquire a mastery of the Celtic language at least.

Much love
Yr affect
MRJ

Notes

1. The excavations at Bury St Edmunds were still uncovering bones. These were the remains of the six abbots, but at this time this fact was unknown, and interested parties were badgering James as to what these bones might be and where they had come from. Other parts of the site were also causing controversy, such as, as indicated here, where the centrepiece of the abbey was originally located. In the end all of these questions were reduced to a moot point by the 'lack of funds' which usually brings a quick death to any archaeological venture (Pfaff, p.140).

2. There is a feeling in this letter that James was beginning to tire
   of his association with Sir Ernest Clarke, and indeed in a footnote
   Pfaff notes:

> There is reason to suspect that MRJ found his association
> with Clarke increasingly tiresome. In January 1903 MRJ
> had suggested 'in the lavatory at Mr Donne's house' (as
> Clarke reminded him) that a new translation of Jocelin
> would be desirable. Clarke, with his typical enthusiasm,
> took up the project, ostensibly in the form of revising the
> translation by Tomlin in 1843, though it soon took on the
> character of a new version ... Clarke's version was
> published in 1903, in the King's Classics series; though it
> was reprinted twice (again in 1903 and in 1907) it was soon
> superseded by L. C. Jane's translation, with introduction by
> Abbot Gasquet published in 1907. (Pfaff p.140)

My Dear Pa

25 October 1903

My Dear Pa,

I yesterday sent off a couple of letters to while away your enforced leisure – with much love and best wishes for Monday.

On Wednesday evening dinner included G Don Henry Jackson, & Kalb Fleisch (what a name) of Berlin, have engaged me to make a catalogue of all the Ancient Medical MSS in Cambridge before the end of November luckily I have done the best part of what is wanted already & I suppose I should have expended more time if they had gone to anyone else.[1]

Thursday morning & afternoon were spent in various meetings & work.

Today I saw H.B.Smith at lunch time [looking] lurking just as ever he is not yet settled in at marital house but is looking for me.

I haven't yet made acquaintance with his wife.

Next week has its crop of syndicates & meetings to be suffered through – Morris is still here, lurking chiefly in my rooms. I just started on a batch of MSS from Pembroke which has luckily enough work to escape from him.

I must steel myself now to ascertain the truth about the committee of Worcester who as I think I told you are desperate to be going to

sell their MSS.[2] If they are, we must employ the strongest language
& protest recurrently in the first instance, and if that fails must not
shrink from telling them what we really think. I expect Woodhouse
to lunch on Tuesday unless I have to go to the library.

Much love

Love on yr bday

MRJ

I looked at the letter of Cromwell to Col. John Lambert. It is not all
autographs: it is a commission given by the prefect, to act as governor
of the city of Worcester in 1651: Sept 8th

Notes

1. Henry Jackson was a close friend of James's since at least his
   undergraduate days, and his time spent in the play *The Birds*.
   Jackson was Regius Professor of Greek at Cambridge, and a
   classicist. His interest in medical MSS and the backing of the
   German family publisher Kalbfleisch in engaging James to
   undertake research into the ancient manuscripts that mention
   this subject are not covered in any extant biographies of James,
   so this is an area of future research for Jamesian studies. As James
   mentions in this letter, the research he was already engaged upon
   gave him a good knowledge as to where these particular MSS
   were and there are a number that mention medical terms,

alchemy, charms and similar matters in the Trinity MSS, St John's College and Corpus Christi and others across Cambridge. It seems, however, that the planned book was never completed, which is unfortunate as it does sound as if the book would have made interesting reading.

2. James had long lamented the buying power of Cambridge in his time at the university noting in his Sandar's lecture on bibliography:

> At no time, I am sorry to say, have the University nor any of the Colleges spent any adequate sums on the purchase of MSS. We find the Bodleian buying the whole Canonici collection in the [18]30s, and a large number of the Meermann books later on. Here we have bought timidly, and by twos and threes, instead of by dozens and hundreds. (Pfaff, p.208)

It is not surprising then to discern a note of melancholy in this letter at the thought of the manuscripts of Worcester coming up for sale as they were unlikely to be prioritised for purchase by any of the Cambridge colleges in James's time.

My Dear Pa

Cambridge University Library –
Rare Manuscripts, ADD 7480-D6-417-561,
Letters from James to his Father & Grace,
1900–1906, King's

King's College (Stamp)

4 February 1904

My Dear Pa,

Not much news again so far. Rain, rain, and a good deal of water
rot. The chief employment has been taking walks with Arthur
Benson who is usually to be got at for this purpose.

Many MSS have also been received sent by Bury.

I haven't got your last letter yet here. I am writing in the
acquisitions room prepatory copying out and later to greet Maisie
Cropper and WMF, I'll answer your letter later if there are any
questions in it to be answered.[1] Til 6 then at it again.

Sherlock Holmes is serialized in the Strand this week. No, I think
& think but I don't think of any further items. We are discussing the
possibilities of adding to the College buildings: some of the rooms
are so badly in need it seems likely that we may add a full lot to
Bodley's Moulding. We are down on the 11th to talk it over.

Much love
Ever yr loving
MRJ

Notes

1. Upon his friend Walter Morley Fletcher's engagement to Maisie
    Cropper in the autumn of 1902, James was to develop a
    friendship with her entire family, the Croppers of Westmorland.
    Originally a mercantile family from Liverpool, they had moved
    to Ellergreen, near Kendal in Cumbria.

    A large and very active family, they welcomed James into their
    clan at one of their frequent informal house parties at Christmas
    1902. Charles James Cropper and his wife Edith hosted a largely
    open house, and it was at this first gathering that James also met
    Sibyl (Billy) Cropper, Maisie's sister, who was destined to be his
    best friend in all of the family.

    Whether Maisie was James's 'Alice' in the same way that
    Lewis Carroll (Charles Lutwidge Dodgson) held Alice Liddell as
    his muse, is worthy perhaps of further research in the area of
    Jamesian studies, especially as Maisie could induce James to do
    all manner of things that were very out of character such as:

    > [Being] induced to sing 'I'm a man wot's done wrong to me
    > parents' and other ballads ... and other unlikely things ...
    > such as visiting the Buffalo Bill Wild West Show (twice: it
    > 'amused me a good deal') and the Kendal Agricultural
    > show. (Pfaff, p.149)

    James and Billy also wrote a sequence of letters to each other
    which were subsequently published in *Cornhill Magazine* by Sibyl
    in November 1939, called 'Letters to a Young Child'. James
    titled his letters to her 'Dear Fellow Scientist' and in return she
    called James 'Dear Dr Apple Pie'. The letters are full of James's
    imaginative portrayals of rooks, and the antics of various cats
    and owls, and demonstrate his power of storytelling.

My Dear Pa

22 June 1904

My Dear Pa,

I am sorry to learn from Gracy that you have a lumbar in your leg again. Is there any book you could fancy from the shops here if you could suggest one to read I could see about it on Friday.

By this time you will probably have heard from St Clair that his Cox is all right.

Owen Smith was up last Friday & we tried to arrange our little programme for the Saturday, we settled to meet at Rugby and move off from there. Johnny Maxwell and he first appeared on Saturday morning & thence to Purfleet Stanford where there would seem to be some plans for Ashby in linc, then to proceed in the direction of Banbury & sleep at Chipping Campen further movements uncertain. But while I should wish to go forth on the Monday, I offered myself up to Lionel ford for the Banbury weekend hoping to make acquaintance with his wife.[1]

I have just got probably the last weekday of this term otherwise I would have envied it.

I trust your leg will allow you to proceed without more delay to Malvern. Could you tell me if you think of a book: if not I shall select one.

Much love

Ever yr loving

MRJ

Notes

1. Lionel Ford had announced his engagement in January 1904, in a letter to his friend. Due to Herbert James's illness in 1903, he said of James senior, 'I fear you will think it must be the beginning of the end.' However, Herbert James rallied, but continued to suffer small and recurrent symptoms of general malaise as noted in this letter. Ford was married that April, urging James to do the same, but this advice went unheeded.

My Dear Pa

Cambridge University Library –

Rare Manuscripts, ADD 7480-D6-417-561,

Letters from James to his Father & Grace,

1900–1906, King's

King's College (Stamp)

26 July 1904

My Dear Pa,

As luck would have it I [ran] came across the Fletchers this morning & though we did not decide a precise date they decided to put it on the calendar between the 6th and 17th August preferably in the vicinity of a week.[1]

This may be a good aid in deciding plans.

I haven't much news. I am working with old leads at collections in the museum, taking stock of them – just the last parts of my Magdalene [M] College MSS & making up missteps of other catalogues.[2]

Because I expect to know I don't know enough to know everything.

Rain has come at last – on Saturday we had sun for the cricket match. I think Christ's were on but they beat us.

J. Harold Clapham is here and seems to like Leeds no more.

Much love

Ever yr loving

MRJ

Notes

1. As mentioned in an earlier letter ('My Dear Pa', 4 February 1904, King's), the Fletchers are Walter Morley Fletcher and Maisie (née Cropper).

2. The Magdalene College MSS (the College always had a large Etonian membership) was begun by James in May 1904. The collection was rather mixed in that some came from the college's Old Library, and some from its Pepys Library and numbered only 33 in all, but included some unusual manuscripts such as a Wycliffe New Testament in English (No.6) containing the only known copy of the Prologue to 1 Timothy, and a finely illustrated fourteenth-century Apocalypse with later commentary in English (No.5 from Crowland). (See Pfaff, p.266.) The catalogue was an ongoing task for James taking him until late in 1909 when the slim catalogue was finally published.

My Dear Pa

Cambridge University Library –

Rare Manuscripts, ADD 7480-D6-417-561,

Letters from James to his Father & Grace,

1900–1906, King's

King's College (Stamp)

19 December 1904

My Dear Pa,

I am glad you like the book I sent. I think the publishers have done it extremely well.

I had to go to town on [la] Thursday and on Friday last week: Thursday to see the syndicate about the Moulding measurements. Friday to see the McClean bequest.[1] This rather I found to consist of ivories, enamels, Egyptian lacquer, jade bowls, coins, ancient cylinders and other delightful things much that we have not seen before after I saw some of their MSS. The others I shall have to go see at Russ hall early next month if all's well.

Then I went by appointment to see one Fairfax Murray who collects many MSS – he doesn't know how many but believes 200 to 500.[2] He gave me one to take away, I have to see about 15 more which he proposes to read, and explained his intentions of giving them all eventually to the Fitzwilliam. He was a friend of the Middleton's & is a friend of Arthur Benson who also met me there by appointment. This is all extremely pleasant. Fairfax Murray is only anxious that no public notice should be given of his gifts.

Tomorrow I have to go up for the King's dinner annual and I must go and finish my speech which has to be read out aloud without paper & must be known by heart. I have a new paper to read you. I only hashed over a couple of things which I couldn't get. I think on balance the grammar was very good.

I shall hope to appear at the King's supper next week and am about to have a very packed diary over Xmas: the holiday only really begins on the 23rd.

Much love

Ever yr loving

MRJ

Notes

1. The 'McClean bequest' was from the estate of one Frank McClean who died in 1904. He was a collector of antiquarian objects and miscellanea. As F. Wormald and P. Giles noted in *Illuminated Manuscripts in the Fitzwilliam Museum* (Cambridge 1966), he was:

> Civil engineer and amateur astronomer ... well known for his work in spectroscopy and astronomy, and for his benefactions to science ... His activity as a collector of ancient coins, manuscripts, early printed books, enamels, and ivories, was carried on methodically throughout his life, to an ordered plan. He was interested chiefly in the history of artistic development and chose his specimens to illustrate the idea of evolution in art, in accordance with

the scientific climate of his age. His 203 medieval manuscripts raised the total in the museum to over 500 and immeasurably extended both the scope and quality of the collection. (Quoted in Pfaff, p.153)

Pfaff himself noted, 'McClean's bequest, taken as a whole, would have made a distinguished small museum in itself' (p.154).

2. The other bequest noted in this letter was from Charles Fairfax Murray, who had been a workshop assistant of Dante Gabriel Rossetti, the pre-Raphaelite painter, and who had authored a book on the painter. He possessed pictures by Rossetti and manuscripts, plus pictures by others in the celebrated group, such as Millais, as well as works by Hogarth, Turner, Poussin, and many others.

Murray still lived in a house that had previously been occupied by Edward Burne-Jones and had risen from humble beginnings to become someone who could wield this kind of artistic power. Arthur Benson had met Murray through his book on Rossetti, and it was through Benson (as noted here) that James was introduced to the collector. As Pfaff noted, it was perhaps the connection of James to the late John Henry Middleton (former director of the South Kensington Museum) and Benson that predisposed Fairfax Murray's generosity to the Fitzwilliam (p.154).

5:
Provost of King's

My Dear Pa

8 May 1905

My Dear Pa,

Hope springs eternal in the human heart and I learn tonight that some at least are likely to vote for W.D. as provost.[1]

As I have told him it seems the first ray of sunshine that has crossed my path for some weeks: but it may be delusive.[2]

I thought I would at least communicate it to you. I have no time for more, for Mark Sykes is staying with me on his way back to Constantinople.[3]

Much love
Ever yr affect
MRJ

Notes

1. W.D. is Walter Durnford.

2. On 28 January 1905, the Provost of King's, Augustus Austen Leigh, died suddenly, so the race was on to find a successor. James did not see himself as a natural choice, but many who were in a position to decide the matter felt that the choice was between Walter Durnford and James.

   James felt that Arthur Benson was a better candidate, and wrote to him to express this. Durnford had turned the provostship down because his wife was ill. Later, however, he changed his mind and decided to put himself forward for the position after all.

   James was seen by some as a better choice politically, being 'a Kingsman and Etonian' as Walter Headlam put it (Cox, p.154).

   In the end James was appointed Provost, with the vote, according to Arthur Benson, split between James with 25 votes, Prothero with 16, Durnford with 3 and himself with 2. James moved into the Provost's Lodge just after Christmas 1905 (the move was delayed due to repairs that were needed to the large old house). (See Cox, p.153 onwards for a full description of events surrounding the appointment.)

3. Mark Sykes was a friend of James's who had come up to Jesus College in 1897 for what was to be a rather lacklustre university career. He subsequently excelled in the army, however, and became known as a diplomat and world traveller. At this time while staying with James he was stationed at Constantinople as the honorary attaché to the British Embassy.

Dear Mr Murray

Wren Library Archives

Add.Ms.a.606/4

Fitzwilliam Museum, Cambridge (Stamp)

3 July 1905

Dear Mr Murray,

I am conveying to you my delight on Friday when I received here first of all, your splendid gift.[1] It is really a wonderful addition to our collections and is quite a new direction. I will say no more than that.

I am most truly grateful & also will Cambridge be when it realises what you have done for it.

When you have leave will you please put on paper the conditions which you wish to be observed with regards to the manuscript. Preceding the arrival of that, they will be withheld from any on dint of copying

I am yours truly

M R James

Notes

1. Charles Fairfax Murray, as is clear over the course of these letters from the Wren Archive, was a generous benefactor to the Fitzwilliam, and between 1904 and 1905 he gave over 30 manuscripts alone (Pfaff, p.154). The number of manuscripts and paintings he gave was worth a catalogue in itself; however this was never done as a whole document and over the years (oddly) there have only been summary notes produced (see Charles Fairfax Murray at the Wren MSS 1–30), which were authored by first James and later Francis Wormald and Phyllis M. Giles. Looking over all of these notes, the particular manuscript referred to in this letter was a Cistercian antiphoner or ecclesiastical book of hours from north Italy.

My Dear Pa

> Cambridge University Library –
> Rare Manuscripts, ADD 7480-D6-417-561,
> Letters from James to his Father & Grace,
> 1900–1906, King's

> The Lodge, King's College, Cambridge (Stamp)

> 14 February 1906

My Dear Pa,

Many many thanks to you for giving me the tablecloth. Much shall I value it & use it on many occasions.

As expected Lady Donaldson – Alba is here again, putting things down and to rights as a consequence the cat spends the day behind the books in the book case.[1]

I have been doing little of late, but in my amusements in my leisure time I have been describing the McLean MSS. My other achievements have been to host here on the 3rd a Malvern committee meeting on weekdays Saturday to Monday.

I have been also asked to get a kitchen maid.

J.W. Clarke has become a proud father. He and I went to a bad performance (I fear we must say) of Lysistrata last night. I daresay too much use of verse and too much of the parts cut.

> Much love
> Ever yr affect
> MRJ

Notes

1. Although James had moved from his rooms in the King's staircase (the Wilkins Building) in December 1905, and into the Provost's Lodge, the lodge was undergoing improvements, and in February 1906 (when this letter was written) only two bedrooms were habitable.

   Staff for the lodge had been advertised for in August 1905, but a full-time kitchen maid was still being sought, and furniture and supplies, including china, glassware and the tablecloths mentioned here, had to be procured. This saw the 83-year-old Herbert James having to journey to Saxham, west of Bury St Edmunds, to buy second-hand furniture for the lodge, and James had to put up with Lady Alba (Albina) Donaldson's 'help' in advising and supervising the military-style effort to house the new man in his office.

   In the end a staff of five was engaged to make the lodge home for one man and his cat: one butler (Larkins, who does sound rather like a character from one of James's ghost stories), an under-housemaid, a kitchen maid, a housekeeper and a secretary, as James had resisted all advice to secure a 'provostess' to live with him there.

My Dear Pa

Cambridge University Library –
Rare Manuscripts, ADD 7480-D6-417-561,
Letters from James to his Father & Grace,
1900–1906, King's

The Lodge, King's College, Cambridge (Stamp)

28 February 1906

My Dear Pa,

It is indeed some days since we exchanged letters. I think that since I wrote – I have been up to town for a CLU meeting but otherwise inside.

I expect [likely] company on Saturday and it will be very nice if you could come on the week you suggest, beginning with the 17th we have got a great deal to do with the Fitzwilliam selection on the 15th.

I have got the bedroom in full order & it must not be long I think before others are completely sorted.

The cat is extremely vocal protesting the changes in the house – anyone approaching her – she sits on the edge of the table & then runs at a great rate.

I have a faculty dinner here this week.

[The] An honorary degree has been proposed for Mr. Chapman which will please him enormously.

I am in a state of anxiety about it as I have been told there is a likelihood of some committee which would take the head of the Fitzwilliam from him.[1]

If this comes, & is supported by any unpredictable angles I shall advise him to write to the vice chancellor & withdraw: this would put him in a very good position on the whole but I expect that the effects upon him would be severe.

I have had my annual raise given in a letter with my annual report: in a review with a paper in the Caucus next Tuesday – meetings last days.

Much love

Ever yr affect

MRJ

Notes

1. Despite James's misgivings, 'The Faithful Chapman' stayed in his position at the Fitzwilliam, but unfortunately he was not awarded the position he craved, as in 1908 Sydney Cockerell was named as James's successor.

   Although both men remained friends, Cockerell's opinion of James's term at the Fitzwilliam was decidedly unflattering, noting that he thought the display of the pictures at the museum

   > utterly barbarous: good and bad pictures, all schools and countries mixed, were packed together on the walls to a ridiculous height and the Greek and Egyptian departments were a complete and repellent muddle, such little oriental

china as there was being housed with other irrelevant objects in the main Greek room and the cases in the Egyptian room being mostly deplorable improvisations. (Cox, pp.176–7)

Cockerell went further, saying, 'It was a pigsty,' and noted that he felt James 'had absolutely no taste whatever (you only had to look at his house to see that) and he hadn't the least idea how to run a museum. He just looked in occasionally to see if there were any letters.'

James may have had no idea how to actually run the Fitzwilliam, but his record, despite Cockerell's disparaging comments, was actually very impressive. His acquisitions had secured the museum's reputation as a world leader in manuscripts alone, and his additions to its holdings were unprecedented.

Dear Mr Fairfax-Murray

Wren Library Archives
Add.Ms.a.606/2

Livermere Rectory,
Bury St Edmunds
8 January 1905

Dear Mr Fairfax-Murray,

It's all very well (and it is also truly kind) to say I needn't answer your most welcome letter: not when its sentiments are so entirely pleasing, I can't refrain from a round of highly fond thanks.

I am on leave at present for some days, & I am asking my accomplished assistant to advise on the safe arrival of your books.[1]

My gratitude is most warmly given & I hope you will take an early opportunity of taking grace from seeing your gifts in their new home.

Arthur Benson will be at Cambridge also I hope for most of the term and it would give me the utmost pleasure to put you up in college where as you say it brings old memories.

~~[Happy]~~ Pleasant tidings of this and of last year, and also a very happy new year to you.

Yours Very Truly
M R James

Notes

1. See letter 'My Dear Pa', 19 December 1904, King's for notes and James's recollection of the Fairfax Murray bequest to the Fitzwilliam.

My Dear Cockerell

British Library Archive

King's College (Stamp)

6 October 1905

My Dear Cockerell,

Many thanks indeed. I will look up the matter in the direction you indicate as well as I can – but I am never much use at genealogy etc.[1] I was sure that the crucifixion given in [~~Douai &~~] Bury archives was the piece of jute weaved at Douai & it seemed to me lately that it was by one of the authors of the letter. The treatment of the weave confirmed it.

It's absolutely very odd if knowledge such as this could be assumed at a paltry little archive like this: but not impossible.

The verse of 3 and I Bury about which it is written: I see that it is an edition of an old Latin, structured as 'Veisio a llena'. The verses are really the types of the old letters and probably a version of the (jeune died out doing this work). They don't seem to have been abrumbrated. I am afraid I have not made a practice Et eject. It may turn out to be a guide to the locality.

I am quite grateful to those friends who have sent me letters at the time of my election: also I am grateful to Jackson & Webb. But I never expected such enthusiasm because as I said I am no expert & I don't expect that the position will bring any particular happiness.

I hope however that when I am in you will use it as a centre for work.

I am putting together an interesting little book about decoding MSS, I should like to send it to you, but it will be in a smaller type face, due to the financial strictures of the Fitzwilliam I am afraid.[2]

Ever Yours truly

M R James

Notes

1. It is clear from this letter that James and Cockerell enjoyed a
   good working relationship (despite what Cockerell said about
   James's curatorial style of managing the Fitzwilliam – see
   footnote to letter 'My Dear Pa', 28 February 1906, The Lodge,
   King's College).
2. The 'little book' that James is referring to here is his pamphlet
   The Wanderings and Homes of Manuscripts. Although published in
   1919 it is clear from this letter that he had started work on it
   much earlier. His introduction brings the reader straight into the
   room with him in his instruction to them: 'It is my purpose to tell
   where manuscripts were made, and how and in what centres
   they have been collected, and, incidentally, to suggest some helps
   for tracing out their history.' Having read it and referenced it in
   my PhD on James and his ghost stories, I can attest that the
   pamphlet is a witty and erudite little work!

My Dear Pa

Cambridge University Library –

Rare Manuscripts, ADD 7480-D6-417-561,

Letters from James to his Father & Grace,

1900–1906, King's

The Lodge, King's College, Cambridge (Stamp)

27 May 1906

My Dear Pa,

I trust you will be able to come over if not today [~~yen~~] yet on some other day not far removed. We have a lot of activity going on but none that would interfere with you.

Alas alack the cat has succumbed, the vet insists that it has been very resilient. I've buried it in the garden poor dear.

I conceive that J.M.E. McTaggart's theory of your own time is just about the impetus you want. I think he has trusted it to God.

I met the Bishop of Durham at tea the other day. He sends most affectionate regards to you.

The triposes are in full swing. Classics part 1 is over. I hope we may do well therein. Several of the victorious are going to appear with me shortly.

I had the choice of music for the choir on Thursday as I probably told you, however, it will indeed be a satisfaction to get the next three weeks over. I expect that between the terms & the hols I may make my way to Hereford to make acquaintances with Miss Jane McBryde whose mother has taken a house there.[1]

I have no news left except for lots of meetings and meetings.

Much love

Ever yr affect

MRJ

Notes

1. After James McBryde's death in 1904, his wife Gwendolen gave
birth to a daughter, Jane, at the end of that year. James said on
the matter of the baby being a girl, 'I rather regret its sex, but it
must be as it may.' He told the mother, 'I am very glad to hear
from you in person and rejoice that the infant is so thriving. I
wonder when I shall find a moment to look in and make its (her,
I beg your pardon) acquaintance.'

James stood as Jane's guardian and Walter Fletcher was duly
appointed as her godfather. His guardianship made him
responsible for legal matters such as helping to set up a trust
fund, which required his advice just after the birth. As Cox noted,
'He had no choice. His feelings for James made him ever aware
that "it doesn't end here"' (p.129).

Gwendolen moved to her new house, Woodlands in
Herefordshire, with Jane in June 1906. It was here that James and
Walter Fletcher met Jane in that same month, and pronounced it
'a pleasant and interesting meeting' (Cox, p.166).

Dear Sir

Wren Library Archives

King's College (Stamp)

15 November 1905

Dear Sir,[1]

I am sending you documents partly on the suggestion of Mr Shipley – a lengthy document about Edwin Drood.[2] Mainly looking at the form of a report of an imaginary syndicate. If you care to print it. You will probably find it too long for a single issue of the review and I should suggest you dividing it at page 6: I should then quantify the proposition by [~~furthering~~] an account of the discussions of the report, in which some other points might be raised. This I have not yet undertaken.

Yours Faithfully

M R James

P.S. I should think I had better not sign this letter, if you print it.

Notes

1. 'Dear Sir' was actually Walter Lamb, the editor of the *Cambridge Review*, the senior members' magazine. 'Mr Shipley' was Arthur Shipley, the Cambridge zoologist and Fellow of Christ's College.
2. James had become so interested in the unfinished plot of *The Mystery of Edwin Drood*, the last book by one of his favourite writers, Charles Dickens, that he took on the mantle of detective himself to try to solve the mystery of who killed Edwin. This letter details the

beginnings of that idea. The 'syndicate' that was formed afterwards was his contribution; it was printed in the *Cambridge Review*, and then a lecture followed on two evenings, 30 November and 7 December 1905. These evenings took the form of presentations of thoroughly researched forensic accounts of the detective work of 'The Senate of the Syndicate', which had looked into the case of Edwin Drood. Their two-pronged investigation focused on two areas: 1. Did John Jasper succeed in murdering Edwin Drood? (To which the Syndicate found in the negative.) And 2. Who was Mr Datchery? James argued that in an ingenious plot turn engineered by Dickens, Datchery is actually none other than Drood himself. This part of the presentation involved James mimicking a J. E. Nixon type character (see first footnote in the letter 'Dear Mother', June 17 1883, Pitt Club Crest) interrupting his lecture and interjecting with questions as to why Dickens had not been consulted on the matter, to which the vice-chancellor answered that he was sorry to report that due to the sad news of Dickens's death the consultation was impossible. However, he was glad that Dickens had not lived to see the report of the Syndicate.

This presentation led to the formation of the actual Edwin Drood Syndicate in 1909, when James, along with his friend Henry Jackson, Regius Professor of Greek, added it to a successful play for the ADC 'Smoking Concert' in 1907. Jackson's more thorough investigation after the play resulted in a minor monograph entitled 'About Edwin Drood', published in 1911 and reviewed by James in the *Cambridge Review* for March 1911. James assesses Jackson's contentions that Drood was successfully murdered and that Datchery was in fact Helena Landless in drag. James, whilst praising Jackson's argument, stated that he would prefer to think that Drood was not dead and was in fact Datchery. The enjoyable challenge of solving Dickens's last mystery was especially gratifying for James: as his biographer Cox attested, his enthusiasm for Dickens's works never waned.

My Dear Pa

Cambridge University Library –
Rare Manuscripts, ADD 7480-D6-417-561,
Letters from James to his Father & Grace,
1900–1906, King's

The Lodge, King's College, Cambridge (Stamp)

[June 1906]

My Dear Pa,

I'll give you a list of events when I know more. These are pretty much all I have seen:

My own preference is:

Tuesday: Syndicate in P.House

Wednesday – Meeting

Thursday – Museum syndicate at Fitzwilliam

Friday – Rescue committee for buildings at Kings

Sat – College meeting

The minutes are read, Thurs, Fri, Sat

Dinner with Mr. Chapman then discussions from Fri – to Tuesday

Mon 11th – Garden meeting in Fellowes Garden

Tues 12th – Apostles in Chapel, Music & Choir

Weds – College Meeting – A Musician cometh today

I have some of the apostle syndicates Monday & Friday

Then all Syndicates except I have papers in Classical – Extremis:
    which I have to look over between Tuesday the 5th and Monday
    the 11th.[1]

I shall look in on the ADC as one might, I don't expect much.

Much love
Ever yr affect
MRJ

Notes

1. As Esmé Wingfield-Stratford noted of James's time as Provost of King's, 'No one could preside with a more unruffled urbanity over those interminable meetings of the College Council' (Cox, p.163), and looking over this schedule that James had sent to his father, it certainly seems as if James's diary was extremely packed. On taking up his post as Provost he had appointed a secretary, Benjamin Benham, who had been the headmaster of the choir school. Although Benham was feared by the choristers, he had a knack for being able to steer decisions through the decidedly stormy waters of College politics. James also ran a very open house at the lodge, as 'he made it easy for visitors to come and go from the Lodge and placed siphons, decanters, tobacco, and cards out ready in the hall'. This was in part to serve the institution of the College, and also to create the air of 'a family of which the more part consists of the young' (Cox, p.164). However, this may have been to the detriment of his own time, as looking over this list of obligations (and as he noted in this letter) there was not much time for the things James loved, namely his own research!

Dear Sir

Wren Library Archives

King's College (Stamp)

16 November 1905

Dear Sir,

Thank you for your notes. These arrived today having been left in the letter box at the lodge. I am still in my home.

I don't really think I could do much by way of shortening. It is a process that takes time of which I have little: and I feel that to be like a real Report the document should be rather long winded.[1]

I don't mind my initials – but should a little prefer to be anonymous.

Yours Truly
M R James

Notes

1. The report was indeed 'rather long winded'. To provide context here, I am reproducing my own report on James's presentation to the imaginary Syndicate at the committee convening on 30 November and 7 December 1905:

M. R. James had a special affection for the novels of Charles Dickens, to which he was first introduced at Eton. In his self-penned memoirs *Eton and King's*, James wrote: 'The collection of books in Tea-room, called "College Library", contained the whole works of Dickens, which were not on our shelves at home. Upon these I fastened like a leech, and mastered them all ... I put Charles Dickens in the forefront of the accessions to my pleasure which Eton gave for it was wholly new.'

However, the question that needs to be asked is why did *The Mystery of Edwin Drood* hold such a fascination for James? The answer would seem to lie in the unsolvable nature of the mystery lent to it by that of Dickens's death, his death ensuring that the novel took on the air of supernatural fiction with its absent author ensuring the mystery of the novel could never be solved. As Michael Cook notes in his *Detective Fiction and The Ghost Story*, (Basingstoke: Palgrave Macmillan, 2014), there are links between the antithetical forms of the ghost story and detective fiction, both having narrative roots in the earlier century's Gothic and the sensation fiction so beloved of James's time. In the mind of a ghost story writer like M. R. James the novel then becomes a ghost story with no rational end, unless he takes pains to lend order to the chaos by turning detective himself to solve the mystery. As Julian Symonds remarked in his 1951 book *Charles Dickens*, Dickens has as good a claim as Edgar Allan Poe to be called the father of the modern detective story. As Angus Wilson notes, Dickens's earlier plots were not especially well crafted, with mysteries only being unravelled in the final chapters, often – as in *Little Dorrit* – harking back to family relationships contrived well before the action in the novels began.

Indeed, the technical perfections that *Edwin Drood* offers do not – again as Wilson notes – 'belong to the Victorian era', but are rather products of this century's mastery of the detective story form, 'like Conan Doyle's Sherlock Holmes'. Holmes was another fascination for James, as his friend Stephen Gaselee records: 'Apart from Dickens, Sherlock Holmes was among his favourites,' and visitors to James's rooms at King's will remember 'the piles of Penny Dreadfuls and Holmes novels nestling with Dickens in harmony on his bookshelves'.

It was through attempting to solve the mystery of Edwin Drood that James developed key elements that were to feature in his ghost stories. He often utilised the plot devices of detective fiction, such as a series of artefacts as clues, to guide the reader along the path of unmasking the ghostly revenant, such as letters or antique manuscripts, to provide a back story to the present-day action. These devices are present in stories such as 'Mr Humphreys and His Inheritance', where the main protagonist tries to uncover the mystery behind his late uncle's bequest, and his 'A School Story', containing an historical death as well as a present crime – in the form of a body discovered at the bottom of a well, an unsolvable plot device, much like the death of Dickens ensuring that the mystery at the heart of the novel could never be solved.

In late 1905, James put these devices to use himself, turning detective to attempt to solve Dickens's unfinished plot narrative. The results of his investigations were presented to the senior members' magazine of King's College, the *Cambridge Review*, over two weekly evenings, on 30 November and 7 December 1905. As Michael Cox, James's biographer, notes, the document took the form of a report of an imaginary syndicate and 'was couched in the language of real Syndicate reports, which "Monty knew only too well"' (p.179).

James introduced his article with the plot device he often utilised himself in his ghost stories: namely, the sudden appearance of an artefact – in this case his usual copy of the college magazine. He thinly disguised the *Cambridge Review* under the pseudonym of 'The University Reporter'. James's introduction continues: 'There was something very odd about this particular "reporter", the print and paper were the accustomed ones, and as good as ever; but the matter was I felt sure unusual.'

His article then focuses on the section that interested him most – the reports of the Edwin Drood Syndicate. The reports took the form of presentations of thoroughly researched forensic accounts of detective work of the 'Senate of the Syndicate', which investigated the case of Edwin Drood. Their two-pronged investigations homed in on two distinct areas: 1. Did John Jasper succeed in murdering Edwin Drood? To which the Syndicate answered in the negative. And 2. Who was Mr Datchery? James argued that Datchery, in an ingenious plot turn by Dickens, was none other than Edwin Drood himself. James continued, 'That the members begged leave to report':

i. That Jasper on the Christmas Eve in question, after the walk that Edwin had taken with Neville Landless (to view the storm hit river), set upon his nephew with a murderous rage and strangled him with his long black silk scarf.

ii. That in the time of the said attack Mr Drood had upon his personage, secreted probably in his coat breast pocket, Rosa Bud's inherited betrothal ring, gold set with jewels, of which the existence was unknown to Mr Jasper.

iii. That after the attack Mr Jasper concealed the body of Mr Drood in the tomb of Mrs Sapsea after removing from his body the watch chain and shirt pin, which he thought were the only personal effects that Drood had on him. These would not have succumbed to the quicklime that Jasper had put into the Sapsea monument to hasten the decomposition of Drood's mortal remains.

iv. That Mr Datchery, the 'Strange Old Buffer' who made his sudden appearance in Cloisterham in Chapter 18, was actually someone already known, but who was disguising themselves. James summed up the proceedings of the Syndicate at this point in his report as posing two questions:

1. Did Mr Jasper succeed in murdering his nephew Edwin

Drood or did Edwin somehow evade this gruesome end?

2. Who is the disguised personage known to the reader as the 'Buffer, Mr Datchery'?

At this point: then, the syndics as a majority were agreed upon one area; i. Mr Jasper did not succeed in murdering Mr Drood (although later in his review of Henry Jackson's monologue on the Edwin Drood mystery, James admitted this was just his own personal naive hope). This hope for Drood's salvation, as it were, rested on the method of Drood's supposed murder, strangulation, which seems to have been decided upon by Dickens in order to leave a loophole (no pun intended) for some artistic method of escape. To address the issue of survivability, the syndics tried several attempts at strangulation on each other, but only managed to render several of their number unconscious!

The question then arose among the syndics as to why the knife or the bullet was not a better method to have been employed by Dickens, but the Syndicate viewed the absence of these methods as pointing to the fact that Dickens did not ultimately want Drood to come to a bad end. However, the syndics were aware that this was a subjective consideration as Dickens could not now be quizzed on the matter.

James went on to suggest that the syndics drew their conclusion that Dickens did not intend Drood to have actually been murdered by Jasper, since in Chapter 15 Drood's inner narrative concentrates on trying to envisage a life after Cloisterham, perhaps in Egypt as an archeologist, for which he has trained for many years. Also in the pictures which accompanied the monthly instalments of Edwin Drood, one in particular illustrates John Jasper entering a small dark chamber, his lantern beam illuminating a figure standing, which the syndics take to be Edwin Drood. ii. The other matters, James went on in his report, that the syndics intended to illustrate were the mystery of 'The Buffer Datchery's' identity. They drew the conclusion that he was in fact

Edwin Drood, afflicted by amnesia, but driven to solve the mystery of why his memory was missing and how he had come to be in this predicament.

The Syndicate also recommended, James summarised, upon solving the part of the mystery of Drood's disappearance, that, after suffering amnesia as a result of the cutting off of oxygen to the brain from Jasper's savage act of strangulation on his personage, Datchery is in fact Drood, his appearance having aged and his hair having gone white from the assault. Hence, we might say, Dickens's emphasis on Datchery being an 'Old Buffer' is ironic, in that he was in actuality anything but.

The report of the Syndicate led to the actual formation on 3–6 July 1909 of the 'Cloisterham Syndicate', comprising James, Henry Jackson (Regius Professor of Greek at Trinity College, Cambridge) and one of Dickens's grandsons from Trinity Hall, Cambridge. The Syndicate took a journey down to Rochester (Dickens's Cloisterham), Cloisterham Cathedral illustrating the Gothic basis of Edwin Drood with its crypts and tombs adding to the ghostly sepulchral air.

On those dates they examined in detail the supposed reality of various Droodian theories – e.g. What access was there to the crypt? Is there an actual Sapsea monument? What were the geographical points and distance of the vineyard, Durdles's Yard and Minor Canon Corner? James noted, 'We attained clearness on some points but did not hit on any illuminating facts!'

Henry Jackson was sufficiently inspired by the Droodian investigations to write his own monograph, *About Edwin Drood*, published in 1911 by Cambridge University Press. 'Jackson,' declared James in *Eton and King's,* 'considered Drood to be the best thing apart from *The Pickwick Papers* that Dickens ever wrote.' James reviewed Jackson's monologue in the *Cambridge Review* on 9 March 1911. The language James used in reviewing Jackson's monograph was decidedly more academic, in that Jackson's assertions included the idea that Edwin Drood was murdered by Jasper with his 'long black silk scarf' and his body flung over the tower where it fell to the ramparts. Edwin's body was then deposited in a heap of quicklime in the crypt of the cathedral.

Jackson also disagreed with previous declarations that Edwin Drood managed to escape the lime pit. However, James in his review admitted the strength of Jackson's argument, though he 'hoped and preferred to still think that Drood is not dead and is disguised as Datchery'.

To conclude, then, for a mind like James's, which appears to have been that of a natural detective who relished making order out of chaos – amply demonstrated by his devotion to cataloguing manuscripts, such as the medieval manuscript collection at Gonville and Caius – and whose preferred reading material consisted of detective novels by such authors as Conan Doyle and Sheridan Le Fanu, the appeal of solving a tragic real-life mystery such as Dickens's unfinished masterpiece is obvious.

Dickens's influence on M. R. James was, as his work on *Edwin Drood* shows, extremely significant. The episode of the Syndicate's investigation inspired later Jamesian works, because as Julia Briggs found, the protagonist of later James stories such as 'The Story of a Disappearance and an Appearance', and 'Casting the Runes' often uses a series of well-placed clues throughout the narrative, similar to the detective format, to arrive at the denouement of the unmasking of the ghostly revenant. Dickens's last ghostly novel, *Edwin Drood*, with its elements of the detective novel, well-placed clues and the disappearance of its main protagonist, and the ghost story with an unsolvable plot due to the death of its author, was one of the influences behind the later Jamesian ghost stories.

My Dear Pa

Cambridge University Library –
Rare Manuscripts, ADD 7480-D6-417-561,
Letters from James to his Father & Grace,
1900–1906, King's

The Lodge, King's College, Cambridge (Stamp)

23 July [1906]

My Dear Pa,

You will have heard from Broadbent of my various visitors &
meetings while he was here,

I stayed with Broadbent while at Eton: he was in very good form.
Hugh Macnaughten – is very dangerously ill with typhoid. I haven't
heard today how he fares yet.

Since Woodhouse went I have had various other guests, Guthrie
and G. Duckworth & his wife who was Lady Margaret Herbert
(Caernarvon). I had not seen her before & am very glad to make her
acquaintance.[1]

On the Thursday I met Arthur Benson at Lady Donaldson's &
had dinner on the Sunday. Mrs Brown is highly ebullient, well-built
and comfortable.

On Saturday we had the Choir School match, my own score was
four wickets & no runs bowled first ball.

My prospects are to stop here for exactly one fortnight from today.
Then on Aug 6th to start from Norwich with Ramsay, Guthrie and
Beaumont and head out.

I think Guthrie aught to be a very good travelling companion &
only hope we may have fair weather. I have made plans to go to

Denmark. I am much divided in mind between say going to places I saw before or going on to the new ones.

I am working hard at Sidney Sussex Hall, & there is a certain amount of college Business on also.

I have only been able to do about 30 Coptic Manuscripts but they have been the stickiest of all, being in parcels consisting of letters & papers, it is a good prospect however to examine them where they have been located.

I expect more news in a few days:

Much love

Ever yr affect

MRJ

Notes

1. Thomas Anstey Guthrie was a new friend in the James circle, and six years older than James. Strangely Guthrie was also neither an Old Etonian nor a King's graduate but was a well-known literary figure. This trip that James writes about took place in August 1906, and included after many changes of personnel Will Stones' younger brother Ned, Allen Beville Ramsay, James and Guthrie.

   Their trip was to Denmark and Sweden, and there were more trips the next year, and years after. The trips included Guthrie until the fateful last trip in 1922, when he suddenly went very quiet at Uzerche. James confided to his friend Gwen McBryde that he 'guessed it might be a post-card with a pig hunting for truffles which we posted to him at Brantome, but we never knew'. (Guthrie was known to be a bit of a glutton with a well-known fondness for truffles.) But whatever the cause, a permanent coolness developed between Guthrie and this party, and as Pfaff notes this was 'one of the few quarrelsome incidents of James's life' (Pfaff, p.222).

Dear Mr Murray

Wren Library Archives

Add.Ms.a.606/7

The Lodge, King's College, Cambridge

24 March 1908

Dear Mr Murray,

Just a line to introduce the intended letter of thanks from the Master of Trinity, They are of course delighted with the picture.[1]

I am ever your

M R James

Notes

1. The portrait of Matthew Prior, painted by Godfrey Kneller, has long been admired by visitors to Trinity College, with a recent review in the *Observer* saying that this painting 'rises at every level to meet singular intelligence of this living presence. It is by far the best work in the show.' ('Godfrey Kneller's Portrait of Matthew Prior: a Mystery Solved'. trinitycollegelibrarycambridge. wordpress.com/2020/05/06godfrey-kneller's-portrait-of-matthew-prior-a-mystery-solved/– accessed 10 June 2021.)

My Dear Sir

Wren Library,
Special Collections,
Uncatalogued Artefacts

The Lodge, King's College, Cambridge (Stamp)

12 October [19]11

My Dear Sir,

I am very much obliged to you for securing me Mrs Carmichael's letter, and for your very kind promise of a photograph of it also.[1]

I will very much appreciate being able to see it. I cannot think what would have happened years ago, as you said, with the limitations. I can only at this very late date express my disquiet at what would have been a very rude act.

I had always supposed it was so but the Bury scribes must have suspected the legend of it was what Christ had said but Mrs Carmichael puts the matter very well.[2]

Yours Faithfully
I am always
M R James

Notes

1. James as noted in this letter is interested in the work of Amy
   Carmichael, a missionary whose work in Burma (Myanmar) and
   India had received a lot of interest at the time he was writing.
   Her book, *Things as they are: Mission Work in Southern India*, had
   been published to a very sceptical public in 1903. Because of this
   reception various missionaries had been asked to provide
   testimonials on her deeds and mission at the beginning of later
   editions of the book, which was reprinted twice again in 1903,
   twice in 1904 and 1905, and still continues to be available.

   Her letters about her work and her experiences as a missionary
   and her pronouncements on her everyday experiences of
   Christian life were at times controversial, and the preservation of
   her letters even while she was living (she died in 1951) was already
   becoming important, as James's comments on the thought of her
   letters becoming lost or damaged show. He was also (for his time)
   embracing new technologies of preserving artefacts, by asking
   for photographs to be taken of the items that were being collected
   for the archives of the Fitzwilliam and King's.

2. James also discusses a separate item of business here, the Bury
   Archive, which he had catalogued earlier as an ongoing labour
   of love. It seems that the legend of Christ and his resurrection
   had also been contemplated by Carmichael in her letters.

My Dear Lamb

Wren Library Archives

King's College (Stamp)

21 October 1911

My Dear Lamb,

I have the pleasure of conveying to you a vote passed by our council. Their notice to the effect that they desire to send their appreciation of the services rendered to the college by Mr W.R.M. Lamb of Trinity College during the past two years.

I am sorry that the period has come to an end: but glad to be the bearer of a message of thanks.[1]

I am Very Truly
M R James

Notes

1. This is a very nice way of firing someone from their position, it must be said. Walter Lamb was born in Adelaide, Australia, and was later to become Sir Walter Rangeley Maitland Lamb. He was a British classicist and secretary of the Royal Academy from 1913 to 1951. He was also a Commander of the Royal Victorian Order (CVO) and in 1943 became a Knight Commander of the order. He published *The Royal Academy: a short history of its foundation and development* in 1951. Therefore this gentle way of being 'let go' from King's did not affect him!

Dear Mr Murray

Wren Library Archives

Add.Ms.a.606/5

The Lodge, King's College, Cambridge

28 February 1908

Dear Mr Murray,

We are making arrangements with all the speed we may, to hang your delightful gifts: and I think we shall indeed be [~~hang~~] keeping the pictures all together, & shifting that very large & uninteresting Manzuoli picture.

And now I have a delicate favour to ask. I sent the beautiful Prior picture to Trinity, & their administration of it is as ideal as you would wish.'

But, & here is the difficulty: was it our wicked friend Arthur Benson who suggested to you that the picture ought to be at Trinity because Prior was a Trinity man? Well, do you know, he <u>wasn't</u> a trinity man? It is true that Halifax his dear friend was at Trinity & they saw a great deal of each other at Cambridge: but, in fact Prior was at Johns (where they have a good portrait of Prior, bequeathed by himself).

I ought to have known that he was not at Trinity: but I'm afraid I took it for granted that Arthur Benson was right in his facts.

Well, now the Trinity people are very anxious that there should be no misapprehension connected with your generous proposal, & that the fact about Prior should be brought to your notice: in order that you should have the opportunity of reconsidering the matter, if such should be your will. But you must not doubt of their very great gratitude for the kind thought which you have had for them; and should you decide to let the matter stand as it is, they will – I have not the least doubt – gratefully accept this picture & hang it where you desire that it should be hung.

On the other hand (and you must forgive the Museum Director who writes these lines) if you think differently as to the destination of the picture after what I have told you, you know how welcome Prior would be in the Fitzwilliam.

The Master of Trinity asked me to put the fate of the case before you and I have done so & ask you kindly to think over it, & let me know your decision.

I am most gratefully

M R James

Notes

1. Matthew Prior (1664–1721) was a poet and diplomat and a scholarship pupil at St John's College Cambridge, not at Trinity where Arthur Benson mistakenly placed him. This mistake was innocent perhaps, but reading this letter from James there is a hint – however delicately worded – of some mischief. Although Trinity's Wren Library has the portrait of Prior, the reason for this was shrouded in mystery (as Fairfax-Murray's gifts to the Fitzwilliam and the Wren were given under strict conditions that the donor remain anonymous!).

   With these letters (which were in the private collection of the noted book collector Anthony Hobson, until recently) the mystery of Prior's portrait being hung at Trinity was solved. In fact the delicate situation outlined here was resolved, with Murray generously agreeing to gift the picture to the college despite the earlier confusion, with the only condition being that the portrait should hang 'anywhere except in the hall' ('Godfrey Kneller's portrait of Matthew Prior: a Mystery Solved'. trinitycollegelibrarycambridge.wordpress.com/2020/05/06/ godfrey-knellers-portrait-of-matthew-prior-a-mystery-solved/).

Dear Lady Elizabeth

Wren Library Archives

HBS.60.87(2)

The Lodge, King's College (Stamp)

8 August 1915

Dear Lady Elizabeth,

I must send a note of immediate thanks for my very pleasant visit. It is a particular pleasure to me as I told Henry to make acquaintance with the families of my old friends: and without being sentimental, I derived great satisfaction from yours.

I was made right at home by my access to the Lambeth & gardens & no less pleasurable was the enjoyable tour of The Palace, otherwise the day was marred by no incident. I did a reasonable amount of work in the Lambeth building.[1]

Yours very sincerely

M. R. James

Notes

1. James was often included in the family life of his friends, often as a sort of pseudo-uncle. Here he is describing an enjoyable day out with Henry Babington Smith's family to Lambeth Palace, to which he was no stranger, having (as he remarks), done work in the palace on its manuscripts and "their stuff"' (see letter 'Dearest Pa', [May–June] 1899, King's).

   There have been many theories on why James never married, and while working on my PhD this question often entered my mind also. One was that James was a closeted homosexual, but no evidence of homosexuality has ever been found. Neither of his biographers Cox and Pfaff discovered anything to suggest that James had homosexual leanings, repressed or not. There were no letters, diaries or novels to be published posthumously à la E. M. Forster's *Maurice*. On the contrary, Pfaff found letters and diaries to suggest the opposite, and one letter in 1906, although facetious in tone, makes for poignant reading. In it, James details to Sibyl Cropper that he has been going through letters dating back to 1874 and has 'been reading the sometimes hardly civil letters of the 36 "Bright Beings that have at different times declined the offer of my Hand and Heart." These letters are all in an envelope by themselves …' (Pfaff, p.220).

   Cox considered James as a typical product of his time and society, in that where he may have been extremely intelligent and comfortable in the all-male society that was King's, at heart he was almost childish, boyish even. It might be said that James was very guilty of one peculiarly late Victorian and Edwardian social idiosyncrasy: that of refusing to grow into manhood. Here it may be seen that he was in good company, as these boyish traits were observed in many of James's contemporaries, such as J. M. Barrie and T. E. Lawrence. Indeed there has been recent work on

Lawrence especially, detailing his perennial boyishness, the rumours of his supposed homosexuality, and his viewpoint of women as useful for sexual exercise only. Harold Orlans, *T. E. Lawrence: Biography of a Broken Hero* (Jefferson, NC: McFarland & Co., 2002) shows the complicated nature that manhood could espouse in that period.

> When men remain boyish well into middle age, continuing to love pranks and practical jokes, to enjoy making animal noises with children and to seek attention by singing falsetto songs in public, it seems reasonable to interpret this immaturity as symptomatic – in part at least – of a reluctance to grow up. (p.87)

Another biography, that of Robert Baden-Powell, demonstrates that Monty James was not the only complicated boyish Victorian-Edwardian man; in fact he was a member of a community of men who cannot be neatly pigeonholed, as many of his critics have naively attempted.

> This ... fits in the Victorian tradition of what the writer Cyril Connolly (1903–1974) calls 'perennial boyishness' ... It is the theory that childhood experiences were so intense for many men that it came to dominate their lives and to arrest their development. Its symbol was Peter Pan, the boy who would not grow up *(puer aeternus)*, and it implies a longing for a perpetual childhood (Tim Jeal, *Baden-Powell*, p.87).

Certainly James felt at ease in the company of children; he maintained friendships with Stella Cropper's younger sister Billy, even attending The Buffalo Bill Wild West Show with her, to the amusement of his friends. Then there were the stories written for children, specifically *The Five Jars* and the introduction James wrote to his friend James McBryde's children's book, *The Story of a Troll Hunt*.

Many of his friends often commented that even in his later years, he seemed to retain this boyishness and was most comfortable in the company of younger undergraduates. (See S. G. Lubbock, *A Memoir of Montague Rhodes James*, p.21.)

Cox observes that, although in the modern world this may raise questions about James's sexuality, 'this seems a hopelessly inadequate summation of the complex cultural and personal factors behind his resistance to marriage' (p.165).

One such personal factor was that James did not have the independent means to support a wife and the inevitable children that marriage would bring, as for most of his life he was dependent on the two great institutions of his life, Eton and King's, for his board and his every need. Cox details how James wanted a life in the country, in the Queen Anne house of his dreams, but without family means to support this he would never be able to break away from the life of an academic within the bounds of these institutions (p.114).

Cox's argument seems very persuasive, as culturally a man in James's position at that time would have been expected to support a wife financially; there was no question of a wife working to support her husband in the class to which James belonged. There were also the other areas of James's life that he had to consider, not just finances but also familial and cultural expectations. One of the occasions on which James found himself falling in love was with the sister of one of his friends, Stella Duckworth, but his sister Grace and his mother were horrified at the prospect. Stella's stepfather was Leslie Stephen, the critic and biographer (and father of Virginia Woolf), and a noted agnostic.

This was an occasion that greatly troubled James's mother, especially when she learned that her son thought his friend's sister, Stella Duckworth, extremely beautiful. She feared an unsuitable match, in which a pious James might marry a member of the irreligious Stephen clan. (B. W. Young, *The Victorian Eighteenth Century: An Intellectual History*, Oxford: Oxford University Press, 2007 p.177.)

Today family opposition is much less of a consideration, but during James's time it must be remembered that societal position was all important, and to be cast out of that society because of parental disapproval was more feared than today, especially as parents often made the matches that led to marriage. The stigma of an unsuitable match was one that would deter even the most ardent of admirers, and by his own admission James was often shy of the female sex (Pfaff, p.62).

Where he was most at home was in the company of his own contemporaries, in the world of King's and Eton. Reading over the type of activities James and the friends in his set enjoyed rather backs up the statement that James was regarded as boyish.

Conversation at the TAF, the Twice a Fortnight society, was what Monty was pleased to call 'trivial'. There was a great deal of mimicry, with Monty as the leading performer, and there were rags (Cox, p.59).

Rags were where one member would play a practical joke on another, such as hanging a hat on a coal scuttle or the like. The rag would then usually descend into what the members liked to call 'horseplay', where they would wrestle. The wrestling would usually continue into decidedly unmanly behaviour of 'vital grasping'. This behaviour was omitted from one biography for 'reasons of piety'. Today we would see such behaviour as repressed homosexuality, or homoeroticism, except that again viewing the society of friends at Eton and King's in their own setting and taking into account the times, they seem more like schoolboys, not sophisticated decadents like Oscar Wilde or Aubrey Beardsley (Cox, p.55). This is where the application of theories like Eve Kosofsky Sedgwick's 'Homosexual Panic' breaks down.

James's celibate existence seems to make such theories almost redundant. His onetime Eton tutor and lifelong friend Luxmoore summed up the type of feelings that surrounded this society of men in a letter to James in 1917 when the Great War barred countrywide travel.

> The club, the country house and well the chapel for that is
> no parallel – all rolled in one with the added freedom, may
> I say it? We are all alone, of a single sex ... (Pfaff, p.216)

Indeed, the life that James lived seemed to be utterly apart from concerns of marriage and the opposite sex, but when a closer examination is given to the ghost stories, there seems again to be a more complicated issue around gender and sex. As I have previously argued, James definitely had two types of revenants and characters that held his interest, that of the strong female, and the intellectually gifted but slightly feminine male. One need only think of Mrs Anstruther in 'The Rose Garden', 'a stately dame of fifty summers' who is totally in charge of her home and husband, or Mr Dunning in 'Casting the Runes', whose world falls apart when his charwoman and maid develop food poisoning (Cox, p.164).

In his own life he demonstrated this love of strong women in the remark he made to his friend Prothero that he had found an actress playing the part of Peter Pan in a 1905 production who would be fit to be his wife: he found her 'fascinating' (Cox, p.164). This remark would be equally fascinating to us in examining his stories, as the two archetypes of James's fantasy seem to meld in the figure of this Peter Pan, a beautiful boy being played by a strong woman.

James was part of a larger collegiate collective which found women congenial, but only if they lived apart from them. He often had women as friends, like the Cropper sisters, or Gwendolyn McBryde, whose daughter Jane was his ward after James McBryde died (even if he did 'regret her sex' at the birth). James was like many middle- and upper-class Victorian men, who believed in the ideal of separate spheres for the lives of men and women, parallel but separate (Cox, p.129).

In his university he voted against the inclusion of women into the colleges and definitely against the idea of equality within any of the institutions: the privilege of education and parity for women challenged the idea of the privileged all-male bastion and James was certainly one who wanted to preserve the all-male elite (Cox, p.126). Except this argument also breaks down in the face of James's arguments with the academic Jane Harrison, as, while he respected Harrison for her standing as an academic, he also denigrated her stance on mythology, and its challenge to his own branch of academic Apocryphal biblical study. It was the idea of women standing as progress that he seems to have feared, not the fact of them being women (Pfaff, p.255).

Michael Kane noted that in all-male elite societies like James's that were based upon a long Christian tradition of 'brotherhood', the society works from within to emphasise and elevate the pure adoration of manly spirituality, intellect and tradition: so much so that any taint of homosexuality is repressed and the symbolic elevated to the point that homosexuality is seen as weak and is very much discouraged. (Michael Kane, *Modern Men Mapping Masculinity in English and German Literature 1880–1930*, London: Cassel, 1999, p.180.)

This is a world where the older members of the institution are held in high fatherly regard and the members are all seen as brothers. Hence the high regard for older men in Eton and King's, like Luxmoore and Henry Bradshaw. This was a world where the taint of homosexuality did not even have a label, until the article written by W. T. Stead in the *Pall Mall Gazette*, which led to the Labouchere Amendment that made 'gross indecency' a crime in the United Kingdom in 1885. (Graham Robb, *Strangers, Homosexual Love In The Nineteenth Century*, London: Picador, 2003, p.95)

It was the spotlight thrown onto this hidden world which had alienated the public and made a moral stigma out of a whole group of society: whereas as a group homosexual men had always existed, now they were a stigmatised group.

James's friends the Benson brothers were homosexual, as were other Cambridge acquaintances such as E. M. Forster, but at the time closeted: the point needs to be argued that, as in much of Edwardian society, these facts were known just not discussed. As Michael Cook argues, 'What is more important is the way in which the scandals ... publicized the existence of homosexual subcultures and made them into a matter for mainstream politics' (p.67).

Stead went so far as to say in his article that if this label was to be believed in its entirety then there would be a mass exodus from the old all-male bastions of Eton, Harrow, Winchester, Rugby and the two universities of Oxford and Cambridge to the prisons of the country. This old-fashioned world, where sexuality did not really have a place, was the reality I would argue that James preferred to inhabit, even if he took pains to ignore the actual world that he occupied himself.

In that era although homosexuality was punishable by law, there was still an underground culture, coded and hidden but very much alive for the men who inhabited that milieu. Their daily lives had to be discreet in order not to draw attention to their lifestyle. Chris White illustrates the everyday world that they moved in and inhabited, remarking that it is possible 'to construct a map of homosexual London, marking the places where these men could meet one another' (Chris White (ed.), *Nineteenth-Century Writings on Homosexuality*, London: Routledge, 2002, p.327). While many of James's friends and acquaintances at Cambridge were homosexual, there is nothing to show that James was part of this world, or even actually aware of it.

His relationships with women also point to this unworldliness. He almost seemed to hold women in high esteem but was intimidated by them to the point of sometimes outward avoidance. Shane Leslie, in a recollection of James, said that in the Cambridge undergraduate magazine, *The Granta*, there was a biographical article about James that mentioned one particular incident which is indicative of this:

> Apparently three weird sisters visited him in his rooms, probably on charitable rather than amorous intent. He excused himself by slipping into the inner room and leaving by a window. At any rate the weird ones were left sitting until they gave up hopes for whatever they hoped. (Shane Leslie, 'Montague Rhodes James', in S. T. Joshi & Rosemary Pardoe (eds.), *Warnings to the Curious*, New York: Hippocampus Press, 2007, p.30)

It did not mean however that he was a misogynist; indeed, whenever that charge was brought against him, he would refute it, the incident of the idealisation of the actress playing Peter Pan being just one such refutation. It was rather that the mores of the society in which he was brought up dictated the idea of men and women as different but equal and that their worlds should be kept apart as much as possible. His was the age of Coventry Patmore's *The Angel in the House*, the age where women were seen as the moral and spiritual guardians of their men and their behaviour.

In James's society, outside of their academic duties men usually behaved as very free of any domestic responsibilities:

> Even as a fifty-year-old provost of King's, MRJ shared with his friends on these trips a boyishness (or even childishness) and light-heartedness which might have astonished the wives of MRJ's fellow heads ... Indeed, in a number of fundamental respects, MRJ's life was marked by external changes and discontinuities much less than most people's ... He lived in the same college (and in only three locations within it) for thirty-six years and at either Eton or King's from the time he was fourteen until his death. (Pfaff, p.222)

Indeed, Arthur Benson repeatedly made entries in his diaries about how James would frustrate him with his dichromatic nature, where on 'one hand he was a remarkable man possessed of the talents for knowledge and retention, but who was irritatingly childish to the point of annoyance'. It begs the question then, where would a wife have fitted in with this world? Or even with James's life and character?

Despite James's prodigious talents in the area of manuscripts and biblical Apocrypha and the output of his fiction, he always retained something of a Peter Pan character who cherished the company of his own band of 'Lost Boys'. The same friends he had at Eton remained with him throughout his life. The two institutions who were almost 'Mother' to him always made sure that he was sheltered and fed. Indeed when he came to move into the lodge at Eton after accepting the provostship, he remarked that now he would have to buy his own port, as up until then it had always been on the table at King's (Cox, p.125).

Moreover these two institutions did not demand a huge workload in return (Pfaff, p.340). This meant that James did not really need a wife and home. The college saw that every need was provided for, and in case we forget, a man of his class would always have had servants. In fact, a wife and home, especially children, would have been a much heavier burden than perhaps he was prepared to bear. He was also not the only James child who never married, as his brother Ber remained single and his sister Grace didn't marry until after she was 40 (Pfaff, p.97).

6:
Provost of Eton

My Dear Jackson

The Lodge, King's College, Cambridge (Stamp)

31 July 1918

My Dear Jackson,

It is more than good of you to write. I had your kind message from Beauham and I do value having it in black & white as well, though I feel uncomfortable when I think of the trouble it has caused you.

It is truly a very great pleasure the prospect of being knit up so closely with Eton, which of all places holds perhaps the first place in my affections. But I begin to realise though very imperfectly as yet that it will be a great wrench to go from here after thirty six years.[1] But Cambridge is a place where one can keep a foot, and I refuse to think of this as a farewell. I hope I shall have a chance of seeing you next term.

Notes

1. The reasons for James's decision to accept the provostship of Eton are long and complex and this book of his letters is not a biography of James. But I can say that, considering all the evidence presented by authors including Pfaff and Cox in their biographies of James and B. W. Young in *The Victorian Eighteenth Century*, this decision may have come from the religious divide in Cambridge which had long

been fermenting. This divide is covered by Pfaff (p.332) where he places the reasons for James's decision on the uncongenial atmosphere of King's, which was after the war 'depleted of its young men', and the religious divide which had been evident on James entering as an undergraduate. It had worsened over the years between those who possessed religious faith ('the Godly party') and those who wanted King's to be overhauled and the religious emphasis lessened. One thing, however, was evident: the prevailing orthodoxy, the culture of 'unbelief' in King's at that time, had rendered James's own quiet kind of Anglicanism quite obsolete (Young, *The Victorian Eighteenth Century*, p.184). Indeed, looking at James's personal letters here, and the ones written by him to Gwendolen McBryde, one gains a sense of an increasing reluctance to engage with religion, especially the writing and giving of sermons, which had been up to that time part of his larger work in the community. James wrote to Gwendolen on 11 February 1918:

The nightmare of an Ash Wednesday address at Salisbury is taking shape. I feel sure my views on country church services (which have somehow come to be the subject) will not be wholly acceptable. Still, they asked for views on something and they must just take what's put before them. (McBryde, p.77)

It is evident from here that up until that particular exclamation James's views on the possible reception of his religious ideas had taken on the air of someone who was largely 'out of the prevailing fashion' of the times (Pfaff p.62).

Whatever the reasons (and I expect there were many not just these particular ones), the spilt between the godly and ungodly parties and the dearth of young voices at King's was such that James chose to accept the provostship of Eton and moved there in September 1918.

Dear Lady Elizabeth

Wren Library Archives

HBS 91 214

The Lodge, Eton College (Stamp)

3 August 1918

Dear Lady Elizabeth,

Will you and the boys accept my best thanks for your kind wishes. To be made part of Eton is a very great pleasure as well you know. I am very glad you have good news of him, whom for years I have called HB. Please give him my love when you write. I am sure he is doing splendid work for the country, as he always had by the way.[1] I remember very well that evening with Rhys Davids and how much he impressed me and engaged my goodwill: a very remarkable and I think characteristic product of Eton. I wish I could write more you will imagine I am already behind hand with letters.

Yours very sincerely

M. R. James

P.S. I should like to be instituted as Michael's Patron 1 day I hope it may be managed.

Notes

1. Henry Babington Smith is recorded as having a distinguished military career; in the Great War he held a variety of postings connected with finance, which included being the deputy governor of the British Trade Corporation. He was then appointed to the Order of the Companions of Honour (CH) in 1917. In 1918, around the time that James wrote this letter to Smith's wife Lady Elizabeth, he accompanied Lord Reading to the United States as Assistant Commissioner and Minister Plenipotentiary (a hazardous undertaking then given the frequent attacks on ships in the Atlantic by German U-boats). Smith was later appointed a Knight Grand Cross of the Order of the British Empire (GBE) in the 1920 civilian War Honours for his services in the United States.

My Dear Sir

Fitzwilliam Museum Archives

Ref: MS.64

1972_1_202107_KLY25_MAS

The Lodge, Eton College (Stamp)

27 February 1919

My Dear Sir,

Mr Cockerell has told me of the very great service you have rendered both to Cambridge & to the country at large by making possible the retention of the Isabelle Psalter: and when I asked him if he thought you would object to my writing to you about it, he encouraged me in my wish.[1] I therefore continue to tell you how profoundly grateful I, as a lover of Incunabula, am: What you have done is both generous & far reaching. The book you have saved for posterity is one which it is not possible to value too highly in itself or as a possible source of information to artists and academics yet to come.

I am sure you have earned the gratitude of future generations as well as many of our time.

Believe me

Yours very sincerely

M R James

Provost of Eton

Notes

1. One of the prior owners of the Isabelle Psalter acquired for the museum by T. H. Riches was John Ruskin, who had bought it from the art collector John Boykett Jarman. Ruskin had dismantled the book in order to be able to have better access to its precious contents, and while he had described it as 'A Psalter, containing in its calendar of the death-days of the Father, Mother and Brother of St Lewis', the book in fact was a book of hours and a psalter written and illustrated in Paris for the sister of St Louis IX, the King of France between (estimated) 1252 and 1270.

   Ruskin had kept the dismantled parts of the book in his drawing room, and often ignomiously circulated its leaves among his friends and extended the viewings to other collectors. After Ruskin's death most of the dispersed leaves were collected and reassembled by Joan Severn and Sydney Cockerell and the whole was sold to Henry Yates Thompson in 1904. Thompson then had the psalter rebound.

   The Fitzwilliam Museum (with the help of James as this letter outlines) then acquired the psalter with Riches' considerable generosity. But further machinations were also required in which the Drawing School at Oxford University was persuaded to part with the richly illustrated leaves still in its possession, by the persuasion of a gift of Ruskin's considerable study of Luini's *St Catherine*, some Dürers and enlarged copies of the manuscript. (ruskin.ashmolean.org/collection/8979/object/13559 accessed 24 August 2021, 10.05)

My Dear Sir

Fitzwilliam Museum Archives

Ref: MS.65

1972_1_202107_KLY25_MAS

The Lodge, Eton College (Stamp)

23 February 1923

My Dear Sir,

I was indeed delighted to hear that you had acquired the Boxall-Coleridge collection and am most pleased to think that you intend to make a permanent & accessible donation of this to the museum.[1]

Also, I am very grateful to you for thinking me a proper person for such an introduction. It will not do to pretend to any knowledge of artistic technique or schools – especially Italian – which would qualify me to discuss that side. My expertise is in the aesthetics. I can elucidate this and show what is missing & summarise the development of recent research & direction of the thought process, and about the other copies of the <u>Speculum</u> in British Libraries of which I have some notes.

I rather remember after having to produce a guide for the grisaille speculum (mielot vanoli) in the Hunterian Museum at Glasgow which is about the best existing copy I have seen next to yours but this you may well consider irrelevant.

I hope that there will be no problem in perusing the collection, but I should be very glad of the photograph of the Pavi MS: I have certainly seen them & it would help me to make an expert copy & fulfil your expectations.

I am

Yours most gratefully

M R James

Notes

1. The anonymous *Speculum humanae salvationis*, or 'Mirror of man's salvation', was written in the early fourteenth century. A popular theological work, it survives in some 350 manuscripts, many of which are illustrated. The copy in Glasgow was made in Bruges in 1455. The French translation is a deluxe manuscript on vellum written in a Burgundian bastard script; its 42 illuminated panels were executed with exquisite care and beauty. (www.gla. ac.uk/myglasgow/library/files/special/exhibns/month/ sep2000.html, accessed 26 August 2021, 11.07)

   The *Salvationis*, which James later produced for T. H. Riches, consists of more than 5,000 lines of Latin verse and is richly illustrated. James had originally encountered it in 1889, when he had taken notes on the six copies then extant in the British Museum, and again in 1902 in the Hunterian in Glasgow.

   A few years later another version of the *Speculum* was edited by J. Lutz and P. Perdrizet from a copy made by Jean Miélot in 1448. This rather rare edition was always spoken of by James with great reverence.

   The *Speculum*, therefore, would already seem to have had enough attention and research hours devoted to it as a volume without the further work that would ensue when Riches acquired the *Boxall Speculum*. This had previously been owned by the portrait painter Sir William Boxall and been given to him by Lord Coleridge, from whom Riches purchased it in 1923 for £1500.

   Riches already possessed a small but choice collection of MSS which James hoped would eventually find its way to his museum, so was keen to keep his benefactor happy. He therefore agreed to work on the *Speculum* for eventual publication in a special Roxburghe Club volume based on the new acquisition.

   James finished most of his introduction to the book in two months, as he had already taken the majority of his notes on the volume in 1911 when it was still owned by Lord Coleridge, an indication of just how familiar he was with manuscripts, where they were and their history (Pfaff, pp.312–13).

Dear Mr Riches

Fitzwilliam Museum Archives
Ref: MS.66_1972
(1–2)_202107_KLY25_MAS

The Lodge, Eton College (Stamp)

2 August 1923

Dear Mr Riches

Many thanks for the photographs & the admirable wording.[1] The latter, most deftly substituted, if I may say so, helps enormously, indeed fully explains the sestinas.

I would certainly leave p.32 blank to mark the Greek as well as leaving a blank leaf after p.77 perhaps putting a note in the middle of the page to show call attention to it. I see you have left a leaf blank in the middle after p.77 but there is matching wording there: according to my understanding C has inadvertently been substituted in the 2nd & 3rd verses.

It would be very good to have some pictures from the actual MS. Lutz & Perdrizet by the way work exactly the same lacuna in that copy (XVI.3 – XXIV2) are in P. I fancy they must have mixed theirs up in the two later.

Chapters V, XIV, XXVIII would be good ones to get.

For the Glasgow MS I send the following particulars:

It is no 60 (T.2.IP) in Henderson Aitkens later catalogue – the pictures are 4 on a page. These which I should ask for are 76 12a 20a 40b

Of the British Museum after Harley 203b is much the usual curiosity.

It is on the whole curious to see so few of the scribes have real artistic merit.

Yours is much the best

Believe me

Yours very truly

M R James

Notes

1. This letter to T. H. Riches is a continuation of the work done by James on the *Hunterian Speculum* (T.2.18) in Glasgow. James is referring specifically to the work done by the editors J. Lutz and P. Perdrizet on the *Speculum* in 1907. This rare volume was always treated with respect by him (according to Pfaff, p.313), although here he does seem to be (gently) poking fun (if in a rather dry academic way) at Riches, who seems to be now in the position of being a recipient of James's gentle good humour.

   James also remarks on the lack of artistic merit demonstrated by other predecessors in the area of translating and deciphering manuscripts, especially the works held in the British Museum which he maintained were curiosities for researchers, without real merit.

Dear Mr Riches

Fitzwilliam Museum Archives

Ref: MS.68_1972

(1–2)_202107_KLY25_MAS

The Lodge, Eton College (Stamp)

20 September 1923

Dear Mr Riches

I return herewith your excellent key to the <u>Speculum</u>.

I am just got back to Eton, and anytime you like to bring C when Oxford trusts me with it.[1]

I shall be delighted to see you: and, having regard to the pretty full use of the Tracitus which I trust I will I don't think I need keep this MS very long.

What I shall <u>not</u> be able to supply, as I think I told you is a considered & valuable opinion as to the school style. Will Cockerell do this? or shall I ask Gow (an expert and truly a much better man) who is very much <u>au fait</u> in (and has seen this MS) to write a little?

Yours Very Truly

M. R. James

Notes

1. In his work on the *Speculum* James had employed not only the
   expertise of Cambridge and his own contacts, but also the helpful
   librarians of the Bodleian Library at Oxford University, in
   particular their catalogue of MS. According to E. W. B. Nicholson
   in the entries here, the book was illustrated between 1263 and
   1265 (the area of artistic expertise that James emphasised in this
   letter he did not possess). This note by Nicholson to try to
   establish the provenance of its previous ownership, and whether
   it had belonged to (or was made for) Edward I and his wife
   Eleanor of Castile, seemed to James to be rather inconclusive,
   however, partly because he felt that the colours had been added
   to later by other artists. (For more on this opinion see Pfaff, p.316.)

Dear Lady Elizabeth

Wren Library Archives

HBS.92.42

The Lodge, Eton College (Stamp)

27 September 1923

Dear Lady Elizabeth,

What you tell me is indeed grievous and whatever we fear the worst of news.[1] I do thank you for writing and telling me clearly in the midst of your grief: and I will do all I can that you would wish, all today I am available in town.

Please believe that I also suffer as you do the terrible sorrow and anxiety the measure of the loss which you would expect to feel. If also for you it helps me if ever so little to inquire what I could do to help.

If there were any possibility of communication which I could affectionately manage I would take the opportunity.

Believe me
Your most affectionate
M. R. James

Notes

1. This letter to Lady Elizabeth was a painful one obviously for James; the letter was in reply to the news of his friend's grievous state of health (see the next letter, 'Michaelmas Day', 29 September 1923).

   James had enjoyed a long friendship with Babington Smith; they had been together at Eton, where James had many anecdotes of his friend's behaviour, some of which he mentions in his biography *Eton and King's*. In one incident in particular, James recounts Smith wandering around during a disciplinary meeting, looking into desk drawers and coming up with 'confiscated pistol cartridges, which he dropped by relays into the fire just behind the magisterial chair, with results very discomposing to us all' (James, p.45). They had then gone up to Cambridge University together on scholarships – James to King's, and Smith winning a place at Trinity (see letter 'Dear Smith', Livermere, May 2 1882); theirs therefore had been a long friendship.

   The loss was felt deeply, as James again recounts in *Eton and King's* (p.266). Here we see that he is trying to find a way to help the soon-to-be widow, Lady Elizabeth.

Dear Lady Elizabeth

The Lodge, Eton College (Stamp)

Michaelmas Day
29 September 1923

Dear Lady Elizabeth,

I have seen Michael as he will tell you and made all such arrangements as we immediately are able to at this end.[1] To wit I've sent letters to Henry's Eton and other friends as well as the wider circles I can't yet reach: but as I was saying to Michael just now there is no single institution or department or persons with whom he had to do that was not certainly better and thoughts go to this because he was so exceptional.

Ever your loving friend
M R James

Notes

1. As detailed in the previous letter (27 September 1923), James had felt the loss of Smith deeply, and was the person trusted with communicating the death to the wider circle of Eton friends and colleagues. Smith would have had many friends worldwide, due to his postings overseas in his long career which included Turkey, India, and America, many of whom would have had to be reached by telegram in those days when the thought of long-distance phone calls was still in the future (the first two-way call being in 1926 between Britain and the US, according to a cursory search of the internet).

Dear Mr Riches

Fitzwilliam Museum Archives

Ref: MS.69_1972

(1–2)_202107_KLY25_MAS

The Lodge, Eton College (Stamp)

Michaelmas [19]23

Dear Mr Riches

Gow brought himself and Cockerell to arrange the necessary & I should ask no better than Mr Berenson should do it so please arrange with him.[1]

I believe you should also ask the British Academy for a few samples from their MSS whenever copies of these are available. I shall be able to add descriptions of these to the ones I have written about.[2]

Yours Very Truly

M. R. James

Notes

1. This letter was a further discussion of the issue of the *Speculum* that James worked on for T. H. Riches. It had been decided (at James's suggestion) that Bernard Berenson would be asked to supply a note on the edition, which Berenson had agreed to. Berenson was hardly a speedy writer as his note to the edition did not arrive in proof form for James to read until August 1925. (See Pfaff for further notes on this, p.314.)
2. James had also talked Riches into paying for photographic plates of the various MS consulted for the book.

Dear Mr Riches

Fitzwilliam Museum Archives

Ref: MS.70_1972

(1-2)_202107_KLY25_MAS

The Lodge, Eton College (Stamp)

26 November 1923

Dear Mr Riches

Mr Cockerell & I agree that it will work to select that set of prints which is the lightest in tone – but which that is we are not perfectly sure!'

The fact is that we can detect very little difference between the sets & would willingly acquiesce in either.

Whatever you like to give then would, I am ready to go on with the work.

Yours Very Truly

M. R. James

Notes

1. James had managed to talk his benefactor T. H. Riches into paying for the plates for the book from, no less, manuscripts in Paris (Arsenal 593), the British Museum (Harl, 2838) and Glasgow (Pfaff, p.314). It was plain though that when the (expensive) plating procedure was completed, the sets had little difference between them, and Cockerell and James were both left scratching their heads over the visual difference!

Dear Mr Riches

Fitzwilliam Museum Archives
Ref: MS.71_1972
(1–2)_202107_KLY25_MAS

The Lodge, Eton College (Stamp)

3 December 1923

Dear Mr Riches

I don't think, except for saving time, that the photograph of the Coleridge Speculum would be of much use to me, thank-you.[1]

Also I don't know how exactly the plate would be interesting in itself.

I am here til Friday just after Xmas: then not til Jan 24th. Two days is the most I should want to spend over the hols. If I get it soon I could send you the bulk of the copy pretty well done.

Yours Very Truly
M. R. James

Notes

1. This letter is again in reference to the expensive set of photographic plates that James had managed to talk T. H. Riches into paying for. It does seem at least that he was sensitive to their cost and was aware of making sure that each expensive plate had to have an explanation for its inclusion in the book.

Dear Mr Riches

Fitzwilliam Museum Archives

Ref: MS.72_1972

(1–2)_202107_KLY25_MAS

The Lodge, Eton College (Stamp)

13 March 1924

Dear Mr Riches

I think I have no special engagements any day after Monday except the 20th. I shall be very glad to see & receive the MS. Perhaps you will come to lunch – 1.30 on whichever day you come.

Do if you can.[1]

I don't mean to keep the MS long – only to verify my parts.

Yours Very Truly

M. R. James

Notes

1. Reading this letter, the main impression one discerns is how James was an utterly lovely man, and a gracious host. The little exclamation in the middle of the letter, 'Do if you can' at the thought of a lunch with the museum's benefactor (and by now a friend), is so polite and gentlemanly, and, as James would say, so very Victorian.

Dear Mr Riches

Fitzwilliam Museum Archives

Ref: MS.72_1972

(1–2)_202107_KLY25_MAS

The Lodge, Eton College (Stamp)

13 March 1924

Dear Mr Riches

I am so sorry. I forgot that this Friday my house is to be laid waste by an all-day 'Maundy party' organised by the Ladies of the place & I shall be as much as Noah's dove as can be expected.[1] But Saturday would be all right.

If not could any day next week?

So Yours Very Truly

M. R. James

Notes

1. With popular readings of women in James's day as being 'shrinking violets', to use a popular descriptive term, these women sound more like the central character in Grant Allen's 1895 novel *The Woman Who Did* or the New Woman who was being lampooned in popular culture having been seen as outrageous in the fin de siècle culture of a few years before.

   The women whom James wanted to find new land away from (like Noah's dove) are indicative of the times changing as his life had progressed, as the letters and their time span in this collection have (I hope) demonstrated.

Dear Mr Riches

Fitzwilliam Museum Archives

Ref: MS.73_1972

(1–2)_202107_KLY25_MAS

The Lodge, Eton College (Stamp)

14 April 1924

Dear Mr Riches

I don't know how soon you are to be back: but in case you want to view before I return to Eton (which should be about Apr.30) I want to say that before I went away I locked up the MS.[1] Wrapped in its wrapper as you sent it in one of the shelves over from mess in the college library at Eton. & in it I put my suggested descriptions of all the photographs, and other interesting matters. The present direction in letter B & the back of the intentionality therein.

I hope you will find ~~the~~ what I have written sufficient to elucidate the pictures. It has been very interesting to do it.

Yours Very Truly

M. R. James

Notes

1. James had been on his Easter holiday break at Aldeburgh, 'taking a dose of sea air' (see McBryde p.126), where he visited Martello towers and read a lot of 'detective stories – which I buy daily' and away from the business of Eton. But as this letter demonstrates he was also thinking of the manuscript while he was away; and it does rather sound as if he was looking forward to returning to finish it.

Dear Mr Riches

Fitzwilliam Museum Archives
Ref: MS.106_1972
(1–2)_202107_KLY25_MAS

The Lodge, Eton College (Stamp)

30 March 1927

Dear Mr Riches

Many thanks indeed. I await the volume with great interest according to your kind leave, I will ask this place to send two or three copies e.g., to the Kings & Eton libraries.

I'm indebted to you for asking me to write the introduction, as it gave an opportunity of making myself more intimately au fait with the subject matter of this speculum.

Truly Yours
M. R. James

Dear Mr Riches

Fitzwilliam Museum Archives

Ref: MS.107_1972

(1–2)_202107_KLY25_MAS

The Woodlands, Wormelow, Hereford (Stamp)

7 August [19]25

Dear Mr Riches

Many thanks for sending me Mr Beaumont's proofs – what a fine thing he has made of it (though I am not sure whether he gives any thought to the fact that the author was obviously a German subject). Shall I return the sheets?

If not, I send a note of one or two things that I have noted:

P.55	L	8 p.	Aenaeum,	Aeneun
	L	17	Lassatta	Lassetta
59	L	29	Cavellitti	Cavallitti
64	L		Obsevatv	Observv
68			Mossaic	Mosaic

I look forward greatly to seeing the completed work.

Yours Very Truly

M. R. James

Dear Mr Morris
DRAFT

Fitzwilliam Museum Archives
Ref: MS.124_1978
(1–5)_202107_KLY25_MAS

Fitzwilliam Museum, Cambridge (Stamp)

14 December 1894

Dear Mr Morris[1]

I have the Bond ready, and I have applied for the £200 bond cheque, and hope the leaves of the MS will be ready in a day or two.[2]

I hope to be coming up to town on Wednesday next, to see the Phillips MSS at Sotheby's, there is nothing of artistic merit – to judge from the catalogue but a good deal that interests me in a literary way.

If I brought the leaves with me I don't feel quite confident of being able to get as far as your house: for I see that I shall have a good deal to look at, at Sotheby's.

But perhaps you could send a trusty messenger with a letter to Sotheby's to buy it deliver the leaves and then we

Notes

1. William Morris (1834–1896), designer, author, and visionary socialist (source: www.oxforddnb.com).

2. In the years 1894–95 James entered into (on behalf of the Fitzwilliam Syndicate and the museum) a protracted negotiation for the 'Grey-Fitz-payn Hours'. This book of hours (now MS. 242 in the museum) is a fourteenth-century illuminated book – and an early example of the Horae executed in central England by a group of craftsmen who produced some of the most significant manuscripts of this period. On inspection of the manuscript it can be detected through the heraldic arms which form the illustrations that this book was commissioned for a knight of the Grey family and his wife, a relative of the Cliffords of Frampton.

   In the early thirteenth and fourteenth centuries the tradition was such that books of hours would be commissioned on the occasions of marriages, and this is believed to have been undertaken for the marriage of Sir Richard Grey to Joan Fitzpayn, the daughter of Sir Robert Fitzpayn and his wife Isabel Clifford (see Donald Drew Egbert, 'The Grey-Fitzpayn Hours: An English Gothic Manuscript of the Early Fourteenth Century Now in the Fitzwilliam Museum, Cambridge,' MS. 242, *The Art Bulletin*, vol. 18, no. 4, (Taylor & Francis, Ltd., College Art Association), 1936, pp. 527–39, doi.org/10.2307/3045652.

Dear Mr Morris
DRAFT

Fitzwilliam Museum Archives
Ref: MS.125_1978
(1)_202107_KLY25_MAS

Fitzwilliam Museum, Cambridge (Stamp)

4 December 1894

Dear Mr Morris

The Syndicate met this afternoon again, and a suggestion was made which they asked me to communicate to you. It was this: they will make a partial payment to you and give The Fitzwilliam the leaves, and a life-interest to you in the work.

You could then, as a substitute undertake to keep it ~~interest~~ insured for burglarly *sic* and larceny then if the insurance becomes recusable (a legal euphemism) it could I presume ~~come~~ fall to the museum.

At the time that we discussed this idea no other objection had come to light and this may be a favourable idea.

If you could let me know if this is a good way of proceeding we should meet early next week.[1]

Notes

1. This letter was a draft held by the Fitzwilliam in the archives. Upon reading it, it soon becomes clear that James really struggled to put into words the proceedings of the meeting he had been party to, between the syndics of the museum on the matter of their trying to acquire the Grey-Fitzpayn Hours.

   The amount that William Morris wanted for the manuscript leaves was not the problem. Rather, it was that once the museum acquired this valuable manuscript it was responsible for the insurance costs of protecting it in such a public space. The wrangling that had occurred over this is clear in the draft where James crossed out and reworded the letter which I have painstakingly transcribed here.

   The draft is over six pages of this letter where he has written a line, then crossed it out and reworded it. His embarrassment over the syndics trying to buy the manuscript but also trying to finagle or 'con' William Morris into still bearing responsibility for ensuring its safety through underwriting the insurance costs – which were in those days considerable – is palpable.

Dear Mr Morris

DRAFT

Fitzwilliam Museum Archives

Ref: MS.126_1978

(1)_202107_KLY25_MAS

Fitzwilliam Museum, Cambridge (Stamp)

4 December 1894

Dear Mr Morris

The Syndicate have just met to discuss the ~~leaves~~ matter and I ~~have~~ am now in a position to proceed with an approach to actually purchase the leaves of the Fitzpayn Horae forthwith.

The syndicate are possessed of the opinion that they would like to see the leaves displayed in the museum and your proposal to have the total of £200 for the work is highly satisfactory to us.

There were one or two of our number (heaven help us) who objected to underwriting the MSS.

The syndics suggested in that case that they aught to hand the leaves back, but I thought you should know these objections to the acquisition and in any case I am deeply aware of the advantage you would be offering us with what is a benefaction.[1]

Notes

1. This is a draft of the letter to William Morris from M. R. James
   that I have transcribed, and again the letter bears many, many
   crossings out of entire passages of the same words that James has
   taken time to muse over and reword, really to the same effect, to
   disguise his embarrassment over the proceedings of the meeting
   of the Fitzwilliam Museum Syndics and their avoidance of
   insurance costs.

   William Morris would have been nearly 63 when these
   negotiations would have been taking place, and the sum of 200
   pounds in those days would now have been the equivalent of
   roughly 6,400 pounds today, so it was a good sum of money,
   however the insurance costs appear again (even with the
   settlement of the money to buy the MSS) still to some of the
   syndics to be a matter of worry.

Bibliography

PRIMARY TEXTS

James, M. R., *Eton and King's: Recollections, Mostly Trivial, 1875–1925* (London: Williams and Norgate, 1926)

James, M. R., *The Wanderings and Homes of Manuscripts* (London: Society for Promoting Christian Knowledge; New York: Macmillan, 1919)

SECONDARY TEXTS

Cox, Michael, *M. R. James: An Informal Portrait* (New York: Oxford University Press, 1986)

Jones, Darryl, *M. R. James: A Life* (Oxford: Oxford University Press, forthcoming)

Joshi, S. T. & Pardoe, Rosemary (eds), *Warnings to the Curious* (New York: Hippocampus Press, 2007)

Joshi, S. T., *The Weird Tale* (Austin, Texas: University of Texas Press, 1990)

Leslie, Shane, 'Montague Rhodes James', In S. T. Joshi & Rosemary Pardoe (eds.), *Warnings to the Curious* (New York: Hippocampus Press, 2007), p.30

Lubbock, S. G., *A Memoir of Montague Rhodes James* (Cambridge: Cambridge University Press, 1939)

McBryde, Gwendolen, *M. R. James: Letters to a Friend* (London: Edward Arnold, 1956)

Murphy, Patrick J., *Medieval Studies and the Ghost Stories of M. R. James* (University Park, Pennsylvania: Pennsylvania State University Press, 2017)

Pfaff, Richard William, *Montague Rhodes James* (London: Scolar Press, 1980)

Young, B. W., *The Victorian Eighteenth Century: An Intellectual History* (Oxford: Oxford University Press, 2007)

WEB PAGES

'An Anglo-Saxon Dictionary', ebeowulf.uky.edu/BT/Bosworth-Toller. htm

'Apocalypse illustrations (Latin MS 19)', www.digitalcollections.man chester.ac.uk/view/MS-Latin-00019/accessed 12 May 2021

Britannica, The Editors of Encyclopaedia, 'Darter'. *Encyclopedia Britannica*, 21 Jul. 2014, www.britannica.com/animal/darter-bird accessed 13 January 2021

'Godfrey Kneller's Portrait of Matthew Prior: a Mystery Solved', Trinity College Library, Cambridge, wordpress.com accessed 10 June 2021

'The Great Fight at the Aquarium', https:// picturegoing.com/?s=the+ corbett-fitzsimmons+fight accessed 29 December 2021

'A Leaf from the Psalter and Hours of Isabelle of France, containing Psalm 97', ruskin.ashmolean.org/collection/8979/object/13559 viewed 24 August 2021

Maryport Advertiser, British Newspaper, Archive.co.uk accessed 29 December 2020

'Smallpox and Vaccination Statistics,' *British Medical Journal*, Saturday 12 May 1877, from bmj.com/content/1/854/586 accessed 29 December 2020

Acknowledgements

To everyone who helped bring this book into the light, in particular:

Frank Bowles, Head Archivist of Cambridge University Library Archives; Jonathan Smith, Archivist at the Wren Library, Trinity College, Cambridge; Emma Darbyshire and Nicholas Robinson of the Fitzwilliam Museum; Mukund Miyangar of the British Library; Professor Darryl Jones of Trinity College Dublin; and my editors Katy Guest, DeAndra Lupu and Anna Simpson at Unbound.

The Provost of Eton, Lord William Waldegrave, and his wife Caroline; Matthew and Simon (surnames redacted as they would be rather embarrassed being the gentlemen they both are); and my husband John, or as he is known on Twitter, 'Himself', for listening to all of my mad nervous utterings about this process (for hours, poor thing!).

Also my parents, Hugh Glyn Mainley (Jr) and Jaqueline Mainley (née Swinnerton), and my sister, Jill Anita Phoebe Crocombe, to whom I owe everything.

A Note on the Author

Dr Jane Mainley-Piddock is a British writer, poet, blogger and book reviewer. She specialises in the ghost stories of M. R. James and the literature of the late Victorian period. She blogs on Blogspot as Dr Jane Mainley Piddock, where you will also find her poetry and short stories.

A lover of cats, books and writing, Mainley-Piddock was born in the village of Johnstown near Wrexham. She was educated at Grango School in the village of Rhosllanerchrugog, and being a self-confessed nerd attended Wolverhampton University, Akron University (Ohio), Wrexham Glyndwr University and Aberystwyth University.

Her favourite authors include Irvine Welsh, Anaïs Nin and M. R. James. She is currently working on a new book of M. R. James's notebooks.

Index

Unbound is the world's first crowdfunding publisher, established in 2011.

We believe that wonderful things can happen when you clear a path for people who share a passion. That's why we've built a platform that brings together readers and authors to crowdfund books they believe in – and give fresh ideas that don't fit the traditional mould the chance they deserve.

This book is in your hands because readers made it possible. Everyone who pledged their support is listed below. Join them by visiting unbound.com and supporting a book today.

Peter Bennet

Austin Benson

Adam Bertolett

Leanne Bibby

Steven Robert Bitgood

Hannu Björkbacka

Amanda Black

Meg Black

Christine Blake

Graham Blunt

Rob Bodger

Barney Bodoano

Dr John Bollan

Brad Bone

N. D. Booth

Meg Botteon

Jean-Marc Bouilly-Lila

Neil Brand

Jason D. Brawn

Alex Briggs

Dr Ruth Brompton-Charlesworth

Lucy Brooke

Kenneth Brophy

Paul Brumpton

Keith Brunton

James Bryan

Jenny Bryan

Jim Bryant

Glyn Buckle

Anwen Bullen

Mark Burgess

Thom Burgess

Miriam Burstein

Clare Butler

Mike Byrne

Michael Caines

Tom Callaghan

Joseph Camilleri

Jane Campbell

Nick Campbell

Ramsey Campbell

Gary Carey

Lee Carnell

Lydia Carr

Ashton Carter

Sarah Carter

Andy Castledine

Matthew Cavanagh

Lauren Cercone

Thomas Chacko

KJ Charles

Jim Chase

David Chrichard

Hazel Chudley

Tony Ciak

Tom Clare

John Clark

Jonathon Clark

Roger Clarke

Jess Clenshaw

GMark Cole

Gina Collia

Michael Conlon QC

Andrew Connell

Scott Connors

Andrew Conway

Michael Cook

Sarah Coomer

David Cooper

John Cooper

James Cooray Smith

Robert Cordon Champ

Brian Corrigan

Alex Cortez

Cardinal Cox

Geoff Cox

Sarah Crabtree

Yvonne Cresswell

Paul Crisell

Quinn Croft

Brenda Croskery

Alasdair Cross

Charles Crowther

Bee Culleton

Helen Culyer

Siobhan Curtis

Catherine Curzon

Guy Cuthbertson

Matthew d'Ancona

Penny Dando

Benjamin R Davidson

Michael Davidson

Catherine Davis

Laura Davis

Victoria Day

Clare Dean

Jon Dear

David Demers

Steve Dempsey

Kara Dennison

Chris Denton

Bobby Derie

Daniel Derrett

James P. Devlin

Jeremy Dibbell

Eleanor Dickenson

Evan Dorkin

Sarah Drake

Annie Drynan

Eddie Duffy

David Dunn

Vivienne Dunstan

Joseph Dunwoody

Melissa Edmundson

Peter Edwards

Martin Eggleston

Ellie Rose Elliott

Simon Ellis

James Enge

M Etherton

Dewi Evans

Timothy Evans

David Evans-Powell

Mark Everden

Charlotte Everitt

Sharon Eyre

Leslie Falkingham

Martin Fisher

Nick Fisher

Nick Fitzsimons

Heather Flyte

Adrian Foote

Brian Foster

Robert Freeborn

Uta Frith

Susan Gardiner

Paul Garner

Mark Gatiss

Amro Gebreel

Daniel Gibson

Rebecca Gibson

Matthew Gilbert

Rob Glover

Michael Golding

Philip Gooden

Penny Goodman

Jonathan Goodwin

Katey Goodwin

Terence Gould

Donna Gowland

Alan Graham

Helen Grant

Timothy Granville

Elyse Grasso

Colin Gray

Jacqueline Gray

Jo Green

Sarah Greenan

Jonathan Greenaway

Stephen Griffiths

Lisa Grimm

Suzie Grogan

Nick Groom

Katy Guest

Christopher Guyver

George Hadjipateras

Neil Hall

Thomas Hall

Chris Halliday

Emma Hamilton-Done

Russell Handelman

Nicola Hardy

Sean Harkin

Ralph Harrington

David Harris

Mark Harris

Pete Alex Harris

Stewart Harris

Brandon W. Hawk

Evan Hayles Gledhill

Gregory Hays

Jonathan Head

Graham Healey

Peter Hearn

Jude Henderson

Stuart Herkes

Ken Hesketh

Stephen Hicks

Duncan C. Hill

Sean Hill

Susan Hill

Kenneth Hite

Michael Hobbs

Hubert Hobux

Amy Hoddinott

Feico Hoekstra

Camilla Ulleland Hoel

Dan Hogarth

Richard Hoggett

Daniel Holme

Steven Holness

Stephen Hopkins

Eileen A Horansky

Rachel Hore

The Horrells

Jo Howard

Jonathan L. Howard

Catherine Howard-Dobson

Joanne Howe

Susan Howe

Scott Huggett

A. Hughes

Richard Hughes

Leslie Hurst

Derrick Hussey

Damien Hyland

Sarah Iles Johnston

Nigel Ince

Kaye Inglis

Catherine Jacob

Andrew James

Simon J. James

Chris Jarocha-Ernst

Jim Java

Toby Jeffries

Christian Jensen Romer

Derek John

Tristan John

Caroline Johnson

Derek Johnston

Chris Jones

Darryl Jones

Mark Jones

Philip Gwynne Jones

Rolf Jordan

Ulf Käck

Daniel Kasper

Jessica Lemieux Kaufmann

Donald G. Keller

Cat Kelly

Helen Kemp

Hilary Kemp

Zoey Kennedy

Daryl Kent

Sarah Kent

John Kerr

Dan Kieran

Matthew Kilburn

Robert Killheffer

Andrew King

E. M. Kkoulla

William M. Klimon

Judith Knott

Elizabeth Knowles

Richard Knowles

Janice Kuechler

Stephanie J. Lahey

Yvonne Lam

Steve Lambert

John Lambrinos

Susan Lansdell

Mark Latham

David Lauchlan

Brian Lavelle

Gavin Lavelle

Tony Laverick

Frazer Lee

Simon Lee Ash

Rebecca Leece

Henri Leigh

Richard Leigh

Paul Leone

Johan Leuris

David Lewis

Katherine J. Lewis

Jonathan Light

Chris Lincé

Nikki Livingstone-Rothwell

Giuseppe Lo Biondo

Dan Lockton

Lyn Lockwood

William Lohman

Andrew Lohrum

Nick Louras

Catriona M. Low

Roger Luckhurst

Anthony Lynch

Iain Macmillan

Kenneth Macnab

Jay Mahone

Phil Mahoney

Mr and Mrs HG and J Mainley

Zbigniew Majer

Philippa Manasseh

Kenneth Mann

Steve Manthorp

Anne Marble

Patrick Marcel

Prof Richard Marggraf Turley

Steven Markham

John Marley

Emma Marshall

Tim Marshall

Beverley Martin

Stuart Martin

Marlene Mason

David Matcham

A Mathers

John Matthews

Laura McAtackney

John McChesney-Young

Daniel McGachey

Pauline McKee

Neil McKenna

Mark Mclaughlan

Kit McLellan

Ryan McMahon

Bridget McNeil

Brent Merrill

Matthew Michael

Kizzia Mildmay

Chris Miles

Frank Miles

Larraine Miles

Jonathon Milne

John Mitchinson

António Monteiro

Jim Moon

Lisa Mooney

Gabriel Moshenska

Duncan Moss

Joseph Moudry

Anne Muir

Christopher Murphy

Noel Murphy

R D Murrell

James Mussell

Steve Mynott

Claire Nally

Carlo Navato

Adrian Neesam

David Neiss

Klil Neori

Mark Newbrook

Christopher J Newman

nicholasdouglass

Babs Nienhuis

Maria Nightingale

Loretta Nikolic

David Nixon

Mark Nixon

G.K. Nobelmann

Michael Nolan

Val Nolan

Nicole E. Norelli

Gillian Norgan

Peter Nowell

Geraldine O'Driscoll BA MA PGC

Hannah O'Flanagan

Caoimhe O'Gorman

James O'Neill

Ciara O'Sullivan

Will Ormsby

Alistair Owen

Ruth Paginton

Michael Paley

Edward Parnell

Susan Parrott

Lucy Pasteur

James Paterson

Mary Pauli

David Peak

Gordon Peake

Oliver Pearcey

Mark Pearsall

Rob Pearson

Jan B. W. Pedersen

Christopher Perry Rasmussen

John Peterson

Patrick Petterson

Anne Pettifor

Debbie Phillips

Maria Cristina Phillips

Dan Pietersen

Thomas Pink

Jim Pitts

Kristin Plant

Justin Pollard

Andrew Pope

Ana Portillo

Jane Potter

Ben Prior

Lisa Pritchard

Jae Prowse

Catherine Pugh

Simon Pulleyn

Chris Purdon

Charles Randles

Lauren Ratcliffe

Tina Rath

Janet Rawlings

Amity Reading

Matthew Redhead

Gwendolyn D. Reese

Anthony Reeve

Lydian Reeves

Michael Reilly

S.A. Rennie

Alan Rew

Fraser Riddell

Leslie Rieth

David A. Riley

Philip Rist

Kellie Roach

Dilwyn Ellis Roberts

Dylan Roberts

Sandy Robertson

Louise Robinson

James Rockhill

Robert A. Roehm

Sophie Roell

Edwin Rogers

Ren Rogers

Jason Rolfe

Alejandro Romero

Allan Ronald

Julie Rose

Tamsin Rosewell

William Ross

Trifin Roule

Duncan J. Rule

Michael Rutherford

Paula Ryan

Michael Sabin

Oskari Salonen

Stuart Salt

Malcolm Sandilands

Robert Sankner

Adam Sargant

Jessica Saunders

Andrew Saxby

Bronte Schiltz

Ben Schofield

Janette Schubert

Matthew Scott

Andrew Screen

Luke Seaber

Andrew Seaman

Christopher Searle

Belynda J. Shadoan

Scott Sharritt

Richard Sheehan

Clare Shepherd

Eloise Shepherd

Dearbhla Sheridan

Jane Shillaker

Simon Simmons

Paul Skinner

Debbie Slater

Iain Smedley

Andrew Smith

Eli John Smith

John Smith

Jordan David Smith

Karen Smith

Michael Smith

Katy Soar

Matt Southern

Adam Spellicy

Janet Spittler

Teresa Squires

Clint Stacey

Rachel Stalker

Shawn D. Standfast

Simon Stanley

Ruth Stevens

Thomas Stevenson

Victoria Stewart

Johann Steyn

Phil Stoole

Brice Stratford

Ciaran Sundstrem

Nick Swift

Andrew Tate

Ian Tattum

Andy Taylor

C Geoffrey Taylor

Mike J Taylor

Niall Taylor

Robert Taylor

Elena Tchougounova-Paulson

The Development Team, Unbound

Eddie Thomas

Peter Thomas

Rhys Thomas

Anna Maria Thompson

Helen Thompson
Matthew Thompson
Ben Thomson
Andrew Thomas Thrash
Joanna Tindall
Karl Tomlinson
Paul Tomlinson
Jo Totton
Simon Trafford
Michael Tree
Robert Tunmore
Justin Turner
Kit Turton
Geoff Underwood
Heather Valentine
Elizabeth Veldon
Mark Vent
Helen Vicat
Neil Vidler
Paul Vincent
Martin Voracek
Mark Waddington
Robert Wade
Christopher Wain
Martyn Waites
Adrienne Walker
Greg Walker
Tony Walker
Chris Walton
Carole-Ann Warburton
John Ward

James Warrington
Stephen Watt
Matthew Waugh
Katherine Webb
Stuart Weeks
Liz Weldrake
Richard Wells
Laura West
Lorraine Wheatcroft
Susan White
William Whyte
John Wilkinson
Craig Williams
Derek Wilson
Paul Wilson
Ann Winsper
Stephen Wise
Bethany Witham
Lucy Wood
Fred Woodard
Janina Woods
John Woodward
Chris Woodyard
Martin Wooster
Lucy Wrapson
Diana Wright
Francis Young
Georgia Young
Gregory Zamarski
Nina Zumel